The Smart Guide to

Word

2000

Basic Skills

The Smart Guide to

Word 2000

Basic Skills

**A Progressive Course
for New Users**

Stephen Morris

CONTINUUM

London · New York

Continuum

The Tower Building, 11 York Road, London SE1 7NX

370 Lexington Avenue, New York, NY 10017-6550

First Published 2001

British Library Cataloguing-in-Publication Data
A CIP record for this book is available from the British Library.

ISBN 0-8264-5697-9

Typeset by Butford Technical Publishing, Birlingham, Worcs.
Printed in Great Britain

Contents

Acknowledgments

Windows and Word 2000 © Microsoft Corporation, all rights reserved. Screen displays from Word 2000 reprinted with permission from Microsoft Corporation.

This book is based on *Word 97 Basic Skills* by Sue Coles and Jenny Rowley.

About this book

Aims

This book introduces the basics of Word 2000 and progresses to an intermediate level in a single, reasonably priced volume. The book assumes no prior experience of any word processing package.

This book is written for people who are new to Word 2000, which is an industry standard word processing package. You can use it:

❏ As part of a college course

❏ For independent study

❏ For reference

Although this book uses a business-oriented approach for the practical activities, this approach will be easily adaptable to other situations where documents for other purposes, such as assignments or projects, are being produced.

You may also wish to further your word processing skills using Word 2000 by reading *Word 2000 Further Skills*, which builds on the material presented in this volume.

A note to lecturers and students

This book introduces students to the basics of word processing through a series of applications-orientated exercises. The approach is structured to focus on the end product, whether that product be a letter, memo, advertisement, curriculum vitae, project report, thesis or other document. A series of self-contained sessions takes students through the production of various document types and gradually introduces them to the features and functions of the word processing package. Each session comprises a series of exercises. As each new function is introduced, the book explains both why the function is useful and how to use it.

The approach is designed not only to introduce students to Word but also to offer them a conceptual framework for word processing that will facilitate the development of transferable skills.

The learning material requires little, if any, input by lecturers, and can therefore be used in programmes based on independent learning. Students learn by practising the commands and techniques to produce specific types of documents.

Word 2000 is a sophisticated package including many desktop publishing type features, a graphics package and a draw package. The text is selective and does not deal with all these in detail, but does take students step-by-step to a level at which they can happily use the help system to master further features.

The exercises follow a theme. Many, but not all, of the exercises lead towards the creation of a student report. This report is concerned with the development of a new fitness facility in a leisure centre. In order to minimise the amount of keying necessary to complete the exercises, early exercises create documents that are reused later in the book. By Unit 11 various earlier documents will be drawn together to produce a project report. Later sessions deal with specific topics and facilities that may be used to enhance the report further or that may be used in alternative contexts, such as the creation of a newsletter.

In Word there are often many ways of achieving the same operation. This book offers the quickest and most user friendly means of achieving set objectives. Although at times other methods may also be indicated, preference is given to operations based on the use of the mouse and menu options. This approach makes maximum use of the self-explanatory nature of the menu options and dialog boxes, and does not ask the user to remember key combinations. Key combinations are indicated against menu options in the system, and users may familiarise themselves with these as their experience in using the software develops.

The appendix, *Customising Word*, is intended for:

❑ Those whose Word system has been customised so that it does not use the default settings assumed in this book. (Students should ask lecturers to perform the necessary commands to return their system to its default setting.)

❑ Those students who, having worked through all the units in the book, feel confident enough to create their own settings for Word.

Conventions

The following conventions have been adopted to distinguish between the various objects on the screen:

❑ On-screen buttons and icon names are shown as **Cancel**.

❑ Menu items and dialog boxes are shown as **File-Open**.

❑ Filenames, names of fields, documents or anything else named by the user are shown as *Field name*.

❑ Text which you are instructed to type in yourself is shown as ***Filename***.

❑ Keys on the keyboard are shown as <u>*Ctrl*</u>.

Indicates a tip providing a helpful hint or shortcut method.

 Indicates a cautionary note.

 Indicates a cross reference.

Creating a Document

What you will learn in this unit

In this unit, basic operations that are fundamental to the effective use of Word are introduced. At the end of this unit you will be able to:

- ❑ Start Word 2000.
- ❑ Create a simple document.
- ❑ Save a document.
- ❑ Close a document.
- ❑ Exit Word 2000.
- ❑ Use Word's aids to typing.

Such operations will allow you to construct simple letters and memos.

The documents created in this unit can be further improved by the use of other facilities described in subsequent units.

The operations covered in this unit are essential to the successful creation of any document. For example, it is essential to be confident that you have saved a document before going on to create longer or more sophisticated documents.

Once you are familiar with Word 2000, you will perform most of the operations covered in this and the next unit again and again. The sequence adopted in this unit is significant. Always remember to save a document after you have created it and before performing other operations, such as printing. When you have completed this and the next unit you will have grasped some important basics.

Word 2000 has a number of default settings, such as A4 paper size and specified margins, which you may wish to adjust later in order to change the document's appearance, but for this unit you should accept the defaults. These default settings usually allow you to create your first documents painlessly.

Starting Word 2000

To start Word 2000, click on the Windows **Start** button, then click on **Programs** and **Microsoft Word**.

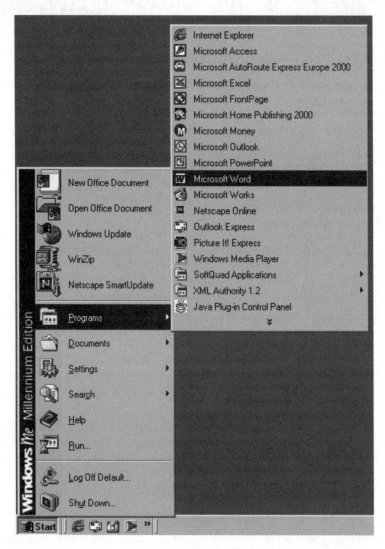

While the software is loading the pointer will be displayed as an egg timer. Word will open with a new document ready for you to enter text. The screen should show the basic Word screen, with an empty document open for you.

A tour of the Word 2000 screen

It is worth studying the Word 2000 screen for a few moments before trying to make use of it. There is rather a lot of information summarised in the next two pages. A quick read should serve to orientate you, but do not expect to remember all of this detail. This section can be used as a ready reference and returned to as necessary.

The Word screen can be formatted in a number of different ways. To make sure that you are looking at the same screen as described in this text, choose **View-Ruler** to switch on a tick against **Ruler** (if it is not already ticked). From the **View** menu move the mouse pointer over **Toolbars** and check that there are ticks by the **Standard** and **Formatting** toolbars.

Now choose **Tools-Options**, then the **View** tab, and make sure that there are ticks against **Horizontal scroll bar** and **Status bar**.

The Word screen that you should now be viewing has the following components:

❏ *Title bar*: shows the name of the document (or *Documentx* if you have yet to name the document).

❏ *Word control menu*: in the very top left-hand corner. If you click on this symbol a menu with commands for sizing and moving the Word window, and closing Word, is displayed.

❏ *Control buttons*: in the top right-hand corner. These buttons allow you to minimise, maximise and close Word. Below the close button is a second close button, which closes the current document only.

❏ *Word main menu*: shows the main pull-down menus, **File**, **Edit**, **View**, **Insert**, **Format**, **Tools**, **Table**, **Window** and **Help**.

❑ *Standard toolbar*: shows a series of buttons that can be used to perform some commands quickly. If you point to a button for several seconds a small box appears showing its name, which gives an idea of its function.

❑ *Formatting toolbar*: shows the character and paragraph formatting in force at the current position of the insertion point. It displays character formatting such as font, size and whether it is bold, italics and so on, and paragraph formatting such as left or right justification. On the left of this toolbar are the font and point size boxes. To the right is a series of buttons for performing common formatting tasks.

The font and point size can be changed by clicking on the list box down arrow to drop down a list of alternatives, and by clicking on one of them. The buttons on the right show the current state of the text and allow it to be changed. For example, to change characters to italic it is necessary to select the characters and click the italic button. The italic button goes in and stays in while the cursor is moving over italic characters.

The style box indicates the style that has been used to format the selection. Styles allow you to format your document more easily.

❑ *Ruler*: gives information about the indentation and tab stops of the selected paragraph. Indents appear as tiny triangles, tabs as shapes indicating their function.

❑ *Status bar*: at the bottom of the screen. It gives information such as the page number and section number of the current location of the insertion point.

Creating a simple document

This exercise takes you into Word 2000, and asks you to open a new document, type in a simple letter and make corrections.

Entering text

Text can be entered via the keyboard. The only important difference between word processing and typing at this stage is that you should not press the *Enter* key at the end of a line. Instead, if you continue typing, the text wraps automatically onto the new line. If you do press the *Enter* key this will prevent the effective formatting of documents later. *Enter* should only be pressed when you wish to commence a new paragraph or to execute a command.

Making running corrections

Simple corrections of one or two characters or words can be made by placing the insertion point beside the character to be amended. Note that Word marks words that it cannot find in its dictionary with a wavy underline but do not worry too much about this at first as spelling will be covered later.

The insertion point can be positioned by:

❑ Placing the mouse pointer where you want the insertion point to be and clicking.

❑ Pressing the arrow keys.

Note that you cannot position the insertion point past the end of a document.

Next apply whichever of the following is appropriate:

❏ Press the *Backspace* key to delete characters to the left of the cursor.

❏ Press the *Delete* key to delete characters to the right of the cursor.

❏ Key in additional characters to insert at the cursor position.

Task 1: Creating a new document

1. Start Word 2000.

Chelmer Leisure and Recreation Centre
Park View Road
Chelmer
Cheshire
CE9 IJS

Universal Gym (Europe) Ltd
Hutton
Brentwood
Essex
CMl3 IXA

17 October 2001

Dear Sir

Health and Fitness Centre for Chelmer Leisure and Recreation Centre.

As part of my studies for my BA in Business Studies, Sport and Recreation, I am conducting a project on behalf of Chelmer Leisure and Recreation Centre.

Chelmer Leisure and Recreation Centre wishes to investigate the options for the enhancement of their health and fitness facilities. Currently I am approaching a number of potential suppliers with a view to collecting information on the range of equipment available in the marketplace. I would therefore be grateful if you would supply me with appropriate publicity literature and equipment specifications, together with price lists.

Thank you.

Yours faithfully

S Leveridge

---

2. Type in the simple letter shown above. Do not forget that you should not press *Enter* at the end of each line unless a new paragraph is required. To create a blank line between paragraphs, press *Enter* an extra time. (Later, we will create the space between paragraphs by changing the line spacing.)

    Make any necessary running corrections.

    Once you have created the letter move on to Task 2, which asks you to save the letter for later use.

Saving a document

To save a document use **File-Save** or click on the 🖫 button on the toolbar.

The first time a new document is being saved this will bring the Save As dialog box onto the screen as shown below.

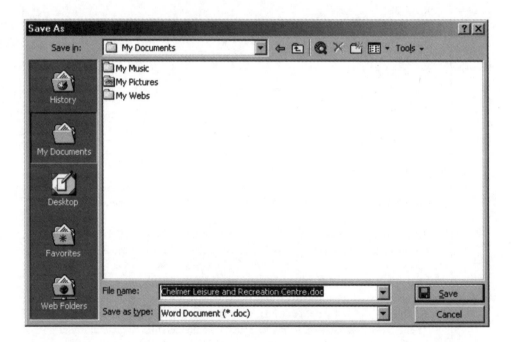

This contains the following boxes:

❏ **Save in:**   This shows the name of the currently selected directory. This needs to be the directory in which you wish to save your file. The downward-pointing arrow allows you to display the directory structure, from which you can select the required directory. You can also create a directory if necessary.

❑ **File name:** This displays the default name: for example, the first few words from the document. You can either accept this or click in the box to modify it.

❑ **Save as type:** This shows the different types of file formats that you may choose to save your file as. Usually the default (Word Document) is acceptable.

For your first document it should be sufficient to choose a directory, enter the filename in the **File name** box and click on **Save** or press *Enter*.

Once you have saved a document it may be resaved on subsequent occasions by using **File-Save**.

 It is good practice to save any document every five minutes or so. Certainly make sure that you save every document before attempting to print it. Word offers an autosaving function, which is described in the Appendix.

More on filenames

In earlier versions of Windows, filenames for Word documents were from one to eight characters in length, optionally followed by a period and a one to three character filename extension. Now, however, Word allows you to use long descriptive filenames. The complete path to the file, including drive letter, folder path name and filename, can contain up to 255 characters.

Any characters may be used except the following: * ? ; \ / : " < >. You cannot use a period except to separate the filename from the extension.

Choose meaningful filenames so that you can easily retrieve your documents later.

Filename extensions are usually used to distinguish between different types of files. For example, document files generally have the extension *.doc*, backup files have the extension *.bak*, and if you have any spreadsheet files created with Excel these will have the extension *.xls*. Generally, there is no need to type the extension because Word automatically adds *.doc*.

Existing Word files are listed in the main part of the Save As dialog, each with a Word document icon next to the filename.

Task 2: Saving

To save the document that you created in Task 1 as *Letter1*:

1. Click on **File-Save**.

2. Choose a directory. If you haven't already created a working directory, do so by selecting an existing directory, clicking on the 🗀 button and entering a directory name.

3. Enter *Letter1* in the **File name** box.

4. Click on **Save**. The file is now safely stored on your hard disk.

    If you wish to save more than one version of a document, you may save the later version of the document under a different filename, as discussed in the next unit.

Closing documents and exiting from Word

Once you have finished working on a document and have saved it you may wish to close it. Closing a document is the equivalent of putting the document away in a manual system. All documents must be closed before exiting Word. If you try to exit with unsaved documents open, Word will ask you if you wish to save and close them. In a Windows application such as Word you may have a number of document windows open at any one time. It is not necessary to close one document before opening a new document in a different window. But new Windows users should be wary of opening too many documents at once. It is easy to convince yourself that you have lost your work when it is merely on a hidden window. So, to start with, close all documents as you finish with them. Documents can be closed by selecting **File-Close** or by clicking on the ☒ button in the top right-hand corner of the document window. When you have closed all documents the application background appears.

When you wish to leave Word, choose **File-Exit**. Alternatively, you may click on the ☒ button, double-click on the control menu box at the top left of the screen and select **Close**, or use the keyboard shortcut *Alt/F4*.

Task 3: Closing and exiting

1. Close the document, *Letter1*, using **File-Close**.

2. Exit from Word by choosing **File-Exit**.

    The document is closed, leaving no documents open in Word.

Using Word's aids to typing

As you type in a document, Word will try to recognise some common text that you type, for example, the days of the week, months of the year, the month and year of a date, and your name (if it knows that you are the owner of the software). As you type the word, Word will guess the completed word and display it in a small box above your typing. Press *Enter* to accept the completed word. If you do not want the word suggested then continue typing and it will disappear.

 Word maintains a list of common words to provide you with these shortcuts, which are known as AutoText. Unit 6 introduces AutoText and you will see how to add words and phrases to the AutoText list.

Task 4: Using AutoText

1. Start Word and open a new document by clicking on the 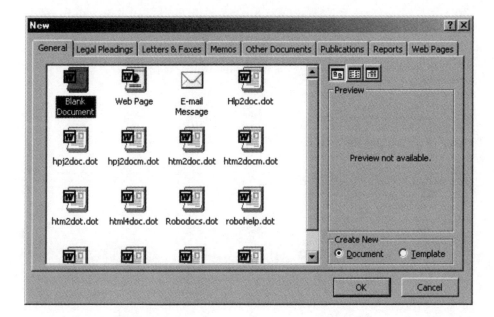 button in the toolbar or by using **File-New** and choosing *Blank Document*.

2. Try typing in the days of the week and the months of the year. Practise accepting or ignoring the completed word.

3. Close the document without saving by using **File-Close** and clicking on **No** in the dialog box. Exit from Word by choosing **File-Exit**.

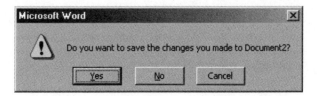

Working with Word Files

What you will learn in this unit

In this unit basic operations that are fundamental to the effective control of documents are introduced. At the end of this unit you will he able to:

❏ Open a document.

❏ Edit a document.

❏ Print a document.

In this unit you will open an existing document, make appropriate amendments and save the altered document under a different filename. By doing this an extra document is created which is a modified version of the original; the original document is unchanged. Normally, documents are saved with the same name following revision, using **File-Save**; however, as Task 1 illustrates, **File-Save As** can create a copy of the document file with either a new name and/or saved in a different location.

What you should know already

Before you start this unit, make sure you can do the following:

Skill	Covered in
Create and save a document	Unit 1

What you need

To complete this unit you will need:

❏ The document file *Letter1* created in Unit 1.

Opening a document

To open an existing document, use **File-Open** or click on the 📂 button on the standard toolbar. This displays the Open dialog box.

The dialog box has a similar layout to the Save As dialog box. Click on an appropriate filename then click on **Open**; alternatively, double-click on the filename. If there are more files than can be displayed in the box, either click on the down arrow or drag the scroll box to view the other filenames.

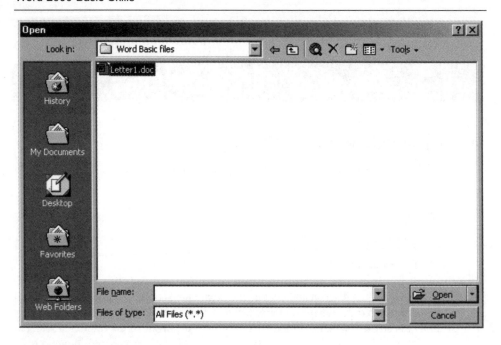

Insert and overwrite

Normally you use the word processor in *insert* mode; that is, the existing text is moved along to make room for any new text. By double-clicking on the OVR button on the status bar at the bottom of the screen you can change to *overwrite* mode, which will allow you to type over existing text. To return to insert mode double-click on the OVR button again. Alternatively, press the *Ins* key to switch between modes. The letters 'OVR' in the status bar appear black when you are in overwrite mode and grey in insert mode.

Saving another copy

An additional copy of a document can be saved, simply by choosing **File-Save As** and entering a new filename. This will create two copies of the document under different names. Alternatively, two copies may be stored under the same name but in different drives or directories. For example, you may wish to save an additional copy to floppy disk by changing to the *3½ Floppy (A:)* drive when saving. To switch to a different drive and/or directory, in the Save As dialog box, open the **Save in** drop-down list box, select the required drive and directory and click on **Save**.

Task 1: Opening and editing a document

This task creates a second updated version of the document *Letter1* while keeping the first version.

1. Start Word 2000.

2. Open the document that you saved as *Letter1* in Task 2 of Unit 1, by using **File-Open** and selecting this file from the list displayed. Check that you have selected the drive and directory in which you saved the file.

3. Add the following paragraph at the end of the text of the letter, before 'Thank you':

    I shall contact you again within a few weeks for more detailed discussions if the Leisure and Recreation Centre Manager feels that your equipment might meet our requirements.

4. Save the new file using **File-Save As**, but this time using the filename *Letter2*.

5. Close the document *Letter2*. You should now have two files, called *Letter1* and *Letter2* respectively. Using **File-Open** again inspect the **Filename** box to check that this is the case. Click on **Cancel** to close the dialog box.

Printing a document

You will normally print a document when it is open and being displayed on your screen. However, you should usually view your document in Print Preview before printing, in order to check the general layout of the page.

The quickest way to create a printed copy is to click on the ⎙ button on the toolbar.

Alternatively, use the **File-Print Preview** command (or click on the ⎙ button) to view the page and then, once in Print Preview, click on the ⎙ button.

Using **File-Print** from either the document view or the print preview will bring up the Print dialog box. Usually you can safely accept all of the default settings, so just click on **OK** and, providing that your printer is on, loaded with paper and on-line, printing will commence.

This is a very simple approach to printing. Below some of the options available in printing are reviewed. There are a number of parameters that can be set. You may wish to skip these for now and return to them later.

Print Preview screen

All documents should be viewed either using **Print Preview** on the **File** menu or the **Page Layout** command on the **View** menu, before being printed.

The Print Preview screen has the following buttons in its toolbar:

⎙	Prints one copy of a document quickly using the current print settings.
⊕	Allows you to zoom in and zoom out.

Displays only one page of the document at a time. Use *Page Up* and *Page Down* to move through the pages of your document.

Allows you to switch between the display of two or more pages on the screen.

57% ▾ Controls how large or small a document appears on the screen. You can enlarge the display to make it easier to read or reduce the display to view an entire page.

Displays vertical and horizontal rulers for adjusting the top, bottom, left and right margins. These can be adjusted by dragging the markers on the rulers.

If only a few lines of your document appear on the last page, you may be able to reduce the number of pages using this option.

Expands the document to fill the screen. Click on this button to display only the previewed page(s) and the Print Preview toolbar. To display all elements click on this button again.

Close Closes the Print Preview screen and returns you to your document view.

▶? ▾ Click on this to display a Help pointer. Click the Help pointer on any item on the screen to show help information.

Print dialog box

The Print dialog box is displayed when the **File-Print** command is used. It allows a number of options to be set.

The dialog box includes the following features:

❑ The **Printer** section shows the current printer, together with details about its status, type etc. Opening this drop-down list will allow you to select an alternative printer if there is more than one printer available.

❑ The **Properties** button takes you to the Properties dialog box. Through this dialog box you may choose from a range of printing options offered by your printer, such as print quality, media size, and landscape or portrait orientation.

❑ **Page Range** shows which sections of the document are to be printed: all, current page, selection (if one is made) or specified pages.

❑ **Print what** shows the document type.

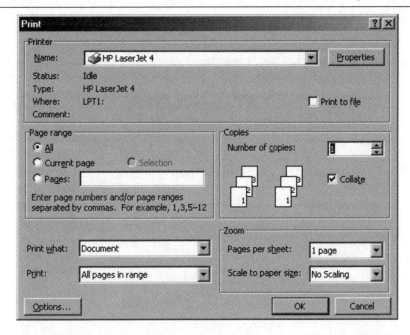

❑ **Copies** shows the number of copies to be printed, and whether they are to be collated.

❑ **Print** allows the choice between all pages, odd pages or even pages to be made. If you wish to print double-sided then this can be achieved by printing all of the odd pages, putting the paper back in the printer (with the page order reversed) and printing all the even pages.

❑ The **Options** button takes you to the Options dialog box. This offers a range of more specialised printing options such as draft output, reverse print order or print hidden text.

Page Setup

Page Setup, on the **File** menu, allows you to set a number of parameters, which specify how the document will be displayed on the page. Four main options are available:

❑ Margins

❑ Paper Size

❑ Paper Source

❑ Layout

Each of these has a separate dialog box, which is displayed when the appropriate tab is clicked. Many of the options in these dialog boxes are self-explanatory and the preview helps to indicate the effect of modifications.

In the **Margins** tab two important characteristics are:

❑ The part of the document to which the settings are to be applied (**Apply to**).

❑ Whether facing pages need to be set with different margins, as in a book, to allow for binding (**Mirror margins**).

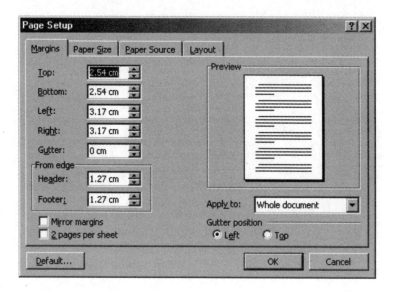

Task 2: Printing

This task asks you to print the document *Letter2*.

1. With the document called *Letter2* displayed on the screen choose **File-Print Preview** to view the document in Print Preview.

2. Select **File-Print** to call up the Print dialog box.

3. Click on **OK** to print the document.

Could you print this document in landscape? Try to set this up using **File-Page Setup** and selecting the **Paper Size** option. View the result on screen with Print Preview.

Document views

Prior to printing your document you will have viewed your document in Print Preview. Word offers several different ways of looking at your document, each of which is suitable for a different purpose. These views are selected either using the **View** menu or by clicking on the icons in the bottom left corner of the Word window. The views are as follows:

❑ *Normal* is the default view. Text formatting is shown, such as line spacing, font and point size, but the layout of the page is simplified.

❏ *Web Layout* is designed to make documents more readable on screen. Documents are increasingly being transmitted electronically and are being read directly rather than being printed. In Web Layout the text is displayed slightly larger and wraps to fit the window.

❏ *Print Layout* shows you how each page of your document will look when printed. You can edit and format the text and see the result on the screen.

❏ *Outline* helps you to examine the logical structure of your document. You can choose to display just the headings. To reorganise a document you can simply drag a heading to another place in the outline, and all associated text moves with the heading. You can also raise or lower a heading's level of importance in the outline.

❏ *Print Preview* (selected with **View-Print Preview**) is similar to Print Layout, but displays whole pages at a reduced size and allows you to adjust various aspects of page layout, but not to edit the text.

You will probably use Normal and Print Layout views most often. Normal view is useful while you get your text typed and corrected, and then Print Layout can be used to adjust the formatting and layout.

Using the **Zoom** command on the **View** menu, or the **Zoom** list box on the toolbar, you can reduce or magnify the display size of a document. The magnification or reduction affects only the screen display.

Task 3: Changing document views

With the document called *Letter2* on the screen, experiment with different document views, first by selecting different views from the **View** menu, and then by selecting **Print Preview** from the **File** menu.

Undoing mistakes

The **Edit-Undo** command is a valuable failsafe. Any time that you issue a command or type or delete some text, you can undo this by issuing the **Edit-Undo** command. This is very useful for retrieving mistakes, and moving back to a previous state. Word maintains a history of the commands you have given it and it is possible to undo a command that was not your last command.

Just to give you complete confidence, there is also the **Edit-Redo** command, which is displayed on the **Edit** menu after you have used **Edit-Undo**, so that you can correct an undo.

Task 4: Using undo and redo

1. Open the document *Letter2* and change 'Yours faithfully' to 'Yours sincerely'.

2. Use **Edit-Undo** to undo the change. Try changing other words in the text of the document, and then undoing the changes.

3. Close this document (without saving it) and open the document *Letter2* again. Change 'Yours faithfully' to 'Yours sincerely'. Next change the date to today's date.

4. To undo both of these two changes, open the undo list box by clicking on the arrow next to the  button on the standard toolbar.

5. Select the last four actions (you may have more or fewer than this depending on what you have done) by dragging the pointer over them and then clicking.

6. Open the redo list box by clicking on the arrow next to the button. Experiment with redoing some of the actions you have just undone. Close the document without saving the changes.

Help

A variety of help is available for Word 2000. There are four main methods of getting into the help system:

❑ Pull down the **Help** menu and select **Microsoft Word Help**. Choose the **Contents** tab if you are looking for an overview of a particular topic. Choose

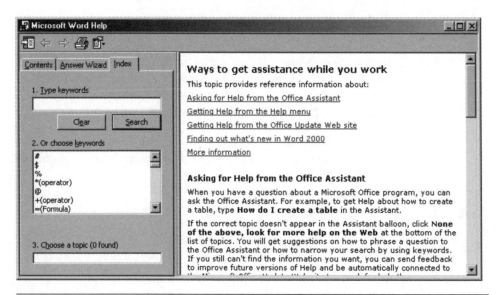

the **Index** tab to look up a specific item. (The Office Assistant must be turned off, as described below.)

❏ At any time you can press the *F1* key to get help on whatever you are doing at that moment via the Office Assistant.

❏ In many dialog boxes there is a **Help** button on the title bar. Click on this, then click on the item in the dialog box for which you require extra information.

❏ Press *Shift/F1*. The pointer changes to an arrow with a question mark after it and can be used to point to anything. Clicking on that object will then bring up help. For instance, in this way you may get help on the meaning of all of the items in a particular toolbar.

The Office Assistant

Click on **Help-Show Office Assistant** button to display the Office Assistant. The Office Assistant is an animated graphic that appears in a window of its own, and if your PC has a sound card it also alerts your attention using various sounds. When you have a question about how to do something you can ask the Office Assistant; for example, 'How do I print in landscape?' To do this click on the Assistant window, key your question into the **What would you like to do?** box and click on the **Search** button.

The Assistant can, if you wish, provide help with tasks as you perform them without the need to ask questions.

You can choose an Assistant to match your personality and as the Assistant is shared by the suite of Office programs, it will be a familiar guide when you are

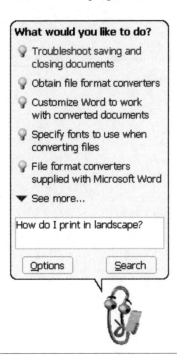

working with an application other than Word. Using the Office CD-ROM, you may select a different assistant, by clicking on the Assistant and choosing from the selection.

To turn off the Office Assistant and use the normal help program, click on the Assistant's **Options** button and remove the tick from the **Use the Office Assistant** box.

Task 5: Using help

This task encourages you to explore the help system and to start to use the Word window.

1. If the Office Assistant is active, turn it off. (Click on the Assistant, click on the Assistant's **Options** button and remove the tick from the **Use the Office Assistant** box. Then click on **OK**.)

2. Click on the **Help** menu on the Word main menu. The pull-down menu is displayed. Click on **Microsoft Word Help** to open the Microsoft Word Help window.

3. Choose the **Index** tab and enter an item, for example 'print', into box 1. Click on **Search**. Choose a topic from box 3. Read the help information displayed.

4. When you have finished close this window by clicking on the ⊠ button in the top right-hand corner of the window.

5. Try choosing the **Contents** tab and looking up spelling and grammar.

6. Click on the Office Assistant and ask 'How do I print in landscape?'

7. You may like to click on the Office Assistant's **Options** button and customise your assistant.

Editing Text

What you will learn in this unit

This unit introduces some activities that will aid document production and presentation. At the end of this unit you will he able to:

❑ Select a block of text.

❑ Move and copy text.

❑ Delete text.

❑ Move quickly around a document.

❑ Find and replace text.

Presentation has an important effect on the reader's initial reactions. When you are producing a document, whether it is for your customers, managers or tutors, good presentation will predispose them to view the document favourably. It is important to proofread your work and make amendments, if necessary, using the techniques introduced in this unit.

What you should know already

Before you start this unit, make sure you can do the following:

Skill	Covered in
Create and save a document	Unit 1
Open and edit a document	Unit 2

Selecting text

Text must be selected before its format can be changed. Text selection is also used to mark a piece of text for deletion, copying or other operations. Most of the operations described in this and later modules require text to be selected first.

Don't forget that the word processor will not change anything if you do not select the part of the document you wish to reformat first.

Any area of selected text will be highlighted. The colour of the highlight depends upon the current Windows colour setting. If the Windows default colour setting is used then the highlight is black. The various methods of selecting parts of a document are summarised in the table below.

Selection using the mouse

To select this	Do this
Word	Move the mouse cursor to the word you wish to select and double-click on the left mouse button.
Line	Move the mouse pointer into the left-hand edge of the screen (the pointer changes to a white, right-pointing arrow) level with the line you wish to select and click the left button.
Several lines of text	Move the mouse pointer into the left-hand edge of the screen, level with the first line you wish to select, click and drag downwards until the last line is selected.
Sentence	Hold down the *Ctrl* key and click anywhere in the sentence.
Paragraph	Move the mouse cursor into the left-hand edge, level with the paragraph you wish to select, and double-click the left button. Alternatively, you may triple click anywhere in the paragraph.
Whole document	Move the mouse cursor into the left-hand edge, press the *Ctrl* key and click the left-hand mouse button or, alternatively, while the pointer is at the left edge, triple click or use **Edit-Select All**.
Section of your choice	Move the mouse cursor to the beginning of the section, click the left mouse button and, while holding it down, drag the cursor to the end of the section.
	Note: You may switch whole word selection on or off by customising Word (see the Appendix).
Undoing a selection	Move the mouse pointer anywhere in the document and click the left button.
Adjusting a selection	Hold down the *Shift* key and click at the point where you wish the selection to end.
	Note: If you initially selected whole units of text, e.g. lines or paragraphs, then the selection will expand or contract by these units.

Selection using the keyboard

Move the insertion point to the place in your document where you wish the selection to begin, hold down the *Shift* key and use the direction arrow keys to move the insertion point to the end of your selection.

To adjust the selection, hold down the _Shift_ key and using the direction arrow keys expand or contract your selection. To cancel your selection press an arrow key without holding down the _Shift_ key.

Task 1: Selecting text

Key in the following text, which is the terms of reference for a report, and save it as _Terms of Reference_.

Terms of reference

This feasibility study looks at a complete refurbishment of the multi-gym at Chelmer Leisure and Recreation Centre. A wide variety of equipment could be offered in a modern fitness suite. This equipment would be a vast improvement on the existing equipment. Various equipment manufacturers have been approached and three have submitted proposals for refurbishment. This report considers each of the proposals received.

The companies from which proposals have been received are:

UNIVERSAL GYM (EUROPE) LTD
ATLANTA SPORTS INDUSTRIES LTD
PHYSIQUE TRAINING EQUIPMENT LTD

Each proposal consists of a list of equipment and plans for the fitness room, plus costings. The proposals are detailed and analysed in the report. The result of the analysis of the proposals will be a recommendation for the best option.

The report will then consider how a new fitness suite would affect the centre's usage. It will also consider ways in which the new facility should be marketed.

Make the following selections and after each selection undo it.

1. Select the word 'feasibility'. Remember that when you have made a successful selection, the selection will be highlighted.

2. Select the first line in the first paragraph.

3. Select the second sentence of the second paragraph.

4. Select the last paragraph.

5. Select the whole document.

6. Select 'Chelmer Leisure and Recreation Centre'. Experiment with selecting words, lines, multiple lines, paragraphs, the whole document and sections of your choice.

You need to move on to the next and subsequent tasks to make use of these selections.

Moving, copying and deleting text

When a document is being written it is easy to use the word processor to make revisions. Revisions can range from restructuring a sentence to rearranging the order in which paragraphs appear. The word processor's abilities to move, copy and delete text are an invaluable aid to putting thoughts onto 'electronic' paper.

Moving: cutting and pasting

If a section of the document is out of place, whether it is a few words, sentences or paragraphs, then it can easily be moved to the right place. First select the section to be moved and use **Edit-Cut**, or alternatively click on the ✂ button in the standard toolbar.

The selection will disappear from the screen. It is stored in a temporary area in the computer's memory called the *clipboard*. It is important to remember that this is only temporary storage and if anything else is copied to the clipboard then the new overwrites the old. To avoid losing the contents of the clipboard an **Edit-Cut** operation should be followed by an **Edit-Paste** operation as soon as possible.

To insert the information from the clipboard into the document, position the insertion point at the correct place within the document and use **Edit-Paste** or click on the 📋 button in the standard toolbar.

Task 2: Moving – cut and paste

With a new document open type in the following sentence:

> The local government environment is changing fast with new laws and new standards appearing almost every month.

1. Select the portion 'with new laws and new standards appearing almost every month'.

2. Use **Edit-Cut** to remove this portion and place it on the clipboard.

3. Move the insertion point to the beginning of the sentence and use **Edit-Paste**.

4. Tidy up the sentence so that it now reads:

> With new laws and new standards appearing almost every month the local government environment is changing fast.

Task 3: Moving – drag and drop

This is a method of moving which is ideally suited to small selections and small movements: for example, rewording a sentence. First select the section to be moved and then click on the selection and hold down the mouse button. As the pointer is dragged notice that at the bottom of the arrow is a small grey rectangle and also a small grey insertion point which follows the pointer movements. This insertion point is the position at which the selection will be dropped when the mouse button is released.

Type in the following sentence:

> If you wish to reserve a place complete and return the reply slip overleaf please.

1. Highlight the word 'please' and the space before it. (**Hint**: Start at the end of the word and drag the pointer left.)

2. Drag the insertion marker to the end of 'place'.

3. Release the button and the sentence should read:

> If you wish to reserve a place please complete and return the reply slip overleaf.

Copying and pasting

This is very similar to cut and paste except that the selected text remains in the document and a copy of it is placed on the clipboard. The copy that is in the clipboard is available to be pasted into the document.

First select the section to be copied and use **Edit-Copy** or click on the 📋 button in the toolbar. Position the insertion point at the place in the document where the copy is to go and use **Edit-Paste** or click on the 📋 button. The contents of the clipboard may be pasted into the document as many times as required.

Deleting

Normal deleting as a running correction can be achieved using either the *Backspace* or the *Delete* key. However, if a larger portion of the document needs to be deleted then it may be selected and then removed by pressing the *Delete* key.

Undoing

Remember that in any of the above activities, if the required change does not occur use **Edit-Undo** straight away and try again. **Edit-Undo** will undo your last action. Alternatively, click on the ↶▾ button. If you wish to undo more than one action use the undo drop-down list.

Task 4: Copy and paste

Start a new document and key in the following text. Save it as *Centre Introduction*.

INTRODUCTION

The Chelmer Leisure and Recreation Centre is at present a very basic gym. It is used by people from a wide range of socio-economic backgrounds. The majority of people using the centre come from the surrounding catchment area.

It is proposed to apply for Local Council funding for refurbishing the present multi-gym facility into a fitness suite. In recent years little money has been spent on the multi-gym. This has resulted in a decrease in the number of users. Present users of the multi-gym are weightlifters most of whom are male.

The fitness centre offers a wide range of activities. The centre is also an extremely popular venue for aerobics, step classes, keep fit and popmobility. These classes are responsible for attracting a large number of female users to the centre, who, in the event of refurbishment of the multi-gym, would be a large target group. The aerobic-based activities account for nearly half of the total number of users of the centre. It is hoped that with the introduction of a fitness suite, those existing users will also use the new facility.

Using **Edit-Cut** and **Edit-Paste** reword the first sentence of the last paragraph to read 'A wide range of activities is offered by the fitness centre'.

1.   First select the part of the sentence 'a wide range of activities' and use **Edit-Cut**.

2.   Move the insertion point to the beginning of the sentence and use **Edit-Paste**.

3.   The sentence requires some tidying up. Make the first word a capital 'A'. An alternative way in which to change the case of a word is to select it and press *Shift/F3*.

4.   Put a space after 'activities' and type the word 'is'.

5.   Select the word 'offers', use **Edit-Cut**, position the insertion point after 'is', use **Edit-Paste** and change 'offers' to 'offered by'.

6.   Make the 'T' in 'The' lower case.

7.   Reword the fourth sentence to read 'Nearly half of the total number of users of the centre take part in aerobic-based activities'. Save the amended document.

Moving quickly around a document

Normally you move around a document by moving the insertion point. The insertion point can be moved using the arrow keys or by moving the mouse pointer to a certain point and clicking. There are also a number of ways to move quickly to another part of the document. These are summarised in the table below.

Key combination	Result
Home	Moves insertion point to the start of the current line.
End	Moves insertion point to the end of the current line.
Page Up and *Page Down*	Move either up or down by one screen height. The insertion point generally remains in the same position on the screen; however, it is in a different part of the document.
Ctrl/Home	Moves the insertion point to the beginning of the document.
Ctrl/End	Moves the insertion point to the end of the document.
Ctrl/Page Up	Moves the insertion point to the top of the current page.
Ctrl/Page Down	Moves the insertion point to the top of the following page.
Ctrl/←	Moves the insertion point to the beginning of the current word.
Ctrl/→	Moves the insertion point to the beginning of the next word.
Ctrl/g (**Edit-Go to**)	Moves to a particular page in the document. Enter the required page number in the dialog box.

Using the scrollbars

There are scrollbars to the right and the bottom of the document window. Using the scrollbars will allow up, down, left or right movement around the document.

By clicking on the box with an arrow at either end of the scrollbar a small movement in the direction of the arrow will be made. By dragging the scroll box to another position in the scrollbar larger movements can be made. Clicking in the vertical scrollbar has the effect of *Page Up* or *Page Down* depending which side of the scroll box you click. Clicking in the horizontal scrollbar causes movements of a screen width. Note that when scrolling the insertion point remains static.

The two double-headed arrow buttons on the vertical scrollbar will move you to either the previous or next page. In between these, the **Select Browse Object** button allows you to move through your document, using the double-headed arrow buttons, stopping at particular objects: for example, headings or tables.

Finding and replacing text

The ability to search through a document and find a particular section of text, or 'string', and if required replace it with another, is an extremely useful feature. There are varied uses for the Find and Replace options.

By using Find and Replace a mistake such as an incorrectly spelt company name can be corrected throughout a document. Find is useful in proofreading. For example, finding a topic name such as 'fitness centre' will enable all parts of the document that deal with aspects of this topic to be found. This helps to ensure consistency throughout a document.

Find and replace

Finding and replacing allows a particular string to be located and replaced by an alternative string. **Edit-Replace** is used to invoke this facility and the Find and Replace dialog box appears with the **Replace** tab selected.

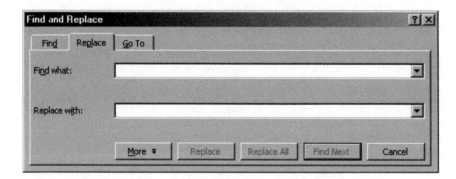

In the **Find what** box enter the text string to be located. This text string may be part of a word, a whole word or several words. The **Find what** list box may be opened to list the previous searches that you may have made and you may select from one of these. In the **Replace with** box enter the replacement string.

To see more options for replacing click on the **More** button which expands the dialog box. Replacing works for the whole document, from the insertion point to the beginning or from the insertion point to the end depending upon whether **All**, **Up** or **Down** is selected in the **Search** box.

Normal searching is not case sensitive so searching for the string 'the' will find 'the', 'The', 'THE' etc. and any words containing 'the', 'The' and 'THE'. To make the search case-sensitive click on the **Match case** option.

If the aim is to find both whole words and any words that contain the search string then leave the **Find whole words only** check box blank. Click on this option to put a cross in the check box if the aim is only to find the whole word. For example, you can search only for the whole word 'place', not words such as 'replace' and 'placement' where 'place' forms part of the word.

The other options provide more sophisticated search techniques.

Once the search string has been found there are three replacement options available:

❏ To replace the search string with the replacement string click on the **Replace** button.

❏ To skip to the next occurrence of the search string without replacing it click on the **Find Next** button.

❏ To replace all occurrences of the search string with the replace string click on **Replace All**.

 Note: The **Replace All** option should be used with caution. Unintentional replacements may occur, especially if the search string forms part of other words.

Find

To search for a particular string choose **Edit-Find** or click on the **Select Browse Object** button in the scrollbar and click on the **Find** icon. This will produce the Find and Replace dialog box with the **Find** tab selected.

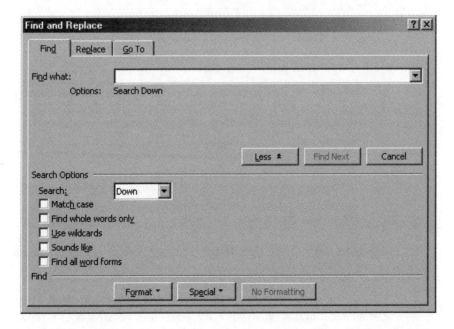

In the **Find what** box enter the text string to be located. Press *Enter* and then click on the **Find Next** button to find the next occurrence of the specified string. To find the next occurrence click on the **Find Next** button again. The direction of the search may be controlled by the choice of the **Search** option.

Task 5: Find and replace

Key the following text into a new document. Save this document as *Centre Usage*.

Usage of the centre

Chelmer Leisure Centre is a fairly small centre, which offers no 'wet' sporting activities. The centre does not have sauna or solarium facilities. Approximately a mile away there is a swimming pool, which offers these facilities.

The centre is well used. In a recent eight-month period over 26 thousand people passed through the centre. On average over three thousand people per month are using the facilities offered by the centre. This gives an average daily figure of over 100 people. However, demand fluctuates depending on the day of the week and whether it was a holiday period.

Popular activities offered by the centre are Step, Popmobility, Keep fit and Aerobics. The figures for people attending these over the eight-month period studied are: Step 5058, Popmobility 4779, Keep Fit 679 and Aerobics 2080. The total number of people attending these activities account for nearly half the total number of people using the leisure centre over the eight-month period studied.

To use the Replace facility:

1. Position the insertion point at the beginning of the first paragraph.

2. Use **Edit-Replace**; in the **Find what** box type 'people' and in the **Replace with** box type 'clients'.

3. Click on **Find Next** and use **Replace**. The word 'people' will be replaced by 'clients' and Word will find the next occurrence of 'people'.

4. Repeat the **Replace** command to replace all occurrences of 'people' with 'clients'.

5. Reposition the insertion point at the beginning of the first paragraph.

6. Use **Edit-Replace**; in the **Find what** box type 'studied' and in the **Replace with** box type 'analysed'.

7. Click on **Find Next** and skip the first occurrence using **Find Next**. This time use the **Replace** command to replace the remaining occurrences of 'studied' with 'analysed'.

Extra features in finding and replacing

In both the Find and the Replace dialog boxes there is a **Format** button. This allows a search string to be defined very specifically in terms of its font, colour and the formatting applied to it.

For example, it is possible to search for the word 'text' where the font is Times New Roman, size 14 and colour green and where it appears in a paragraph that is centre justified.

Finding and replacing special characters

Word allows for many special characters to be located and replaced. A special character is one that usually has an invisible effect upon the document. Examples of special characters include the tab character, the paragraph mark and the page break. Special characters can be made to show by clicking on the ¶ button. Clicking this button again will cause them to disappear.

For example, suppose a piece of text that was originally created by another word processor is imported into Word. At the end of every line regardless of whether it is the end of a sentence or paragraph there is a new line character. In Word a new line character or paragraph mark is only necessary at the end of paragraphs.

To allow Word to perform word wrapping on this piece of text the superfluous paragraph marks will need to be removed. Some will be kept; that is, those that mark the end of each paragraph.

This task can be performed by using **Edit-Replace**. Click on the **Special** button and select **Paragraph Mark** from the list. **^p** appears in the **Find what** box. Enter a space in the **Replace with** box. Click on the **Replace** button where a replacement is required and the **Find Next** button where a replacement is not required, i.e. where there are ends of paragraphs.

Some of the special characters you may wish to find or replace are tab (^t) characters and non-automatic (or *hard*) page breaks (^m).

Task 6: Displaying special character marks

Open the document *Centre Usage* from Task 5 and click on the ¶ button. If you have a paragraph marker at the end of every line you have not been using word wrap properly (see Unit 1).

Note which other special characters are displayed. Click on the ¶ button to remove the special characters from the display.

Task 7: Find and replace

Type the following text into a new document, saving it as *Mouse*.

The mouse is a hand-held device connected to a computer, which can be used as an alternative to the keyboard for issuing commands or instructions. Its shape resembles a mouse with a cable for a tail and buttons for eyes. Unlike a real mouse the cable emerges from between the eyes! The operator's hand grips the mouse between thumb and little finger allowing the first and second fingers to rest over the buttons.

Sliding the mouse over the desktop, ideally using a mouse mat, beside the computer, rotates a direction sensitive ball inside, which in turn causes a pointer to move around the screen.

Commands are chosen from an on-screen menu by pointing to them with the tip of the pointer and usually 'clicking' the left-hand button.

In painting applications the pointer can be used as a drawing tool such as a paintbrush. A palette of colours is available and selecting from the palette puts paint on the paintbrush. It is usual to be able to alter the thickness of the line painted by the paintbrush. There may also be an air-brush tool which creates a spray painting effect.

1. Position the insertion point at the top of the document.

2. Using **Edit-Find** and, searching down through the text, find every instance of the word 'paint'.

3. Position the insertion point at the end of the document.

4. Use **Edit-Find** to find the word 'mouse', searching up through the text.

5. Repeat the search to find every instance of the whole word 'paint'.

6. Using **Find-Replace**, change the word 'mouse' to 'rodent'. Close the document without saving it.

Formatting Text

What you will learn in this unit

This unit focuses on text formatting. Modern word processors such as Word allow a great variety of formatting to be applied to text. This flexibility allows you to develop you own personal style for text presentation. At the end of this unit you will be able to:

❑ Use text attributes (bold, italic etc.)

❑ Select a font (the design and size of the letters).

❑ Alter the margins.

Formatting is used to make the text look appealing to the reader and to draw attention to headings or important points within the document.

With a powerful word processor such as Word 2000 you have at your disposal many choices of text attribute and font. Some typefaces are available in many different sizes. This is another way, in addition to the use of bold, italic and underlined type, in which to highlight or emphasise parts of your document.

What you should know already

Before you start this unit, make sure you can do the following:

Skill	Covered in
Create and save a document	Unit 1
Open and edit a document	Unit 2
Select text	Unit 3

Using text attributes

A character may be printed in **bold** or *italic* type or <u>underlined</u>. Bold type or underlining are often used for headings to distinguish them from the rest of the text. Text attributes are also used to put emphasis on a section of text.

Selection of text attributes using the mouse

As you type you can change the text attribtues simply by depressing the required buttons in the formatting toolbar:

Bold	**B**
Italic	*I*
Underline	U

To depress a button simply move the mouse pointer to it and click. Any subsequent typing will take the attribtues you have set. To switch off the attributes click on the button again. When an attribute is selected its button is a lighter grey than the surrounding area.

More than one font may be used at once, for example ***bold italic underlined*** text.

Selection of text attributes using the keyboard

Formatting may be applied using the keyboard instead of the mouse using the following key combinations:

Bold	*Ctrl/b*
Italic	*Ctrl/i*
Underline	*Ctrl/u*
Word underline	*Ctrl/Shift/w*
Double underline	*Ctrl/Shift/d*

To reformat existing text, first select the text you wish to reformat and then choose the appropriate mouse or keyboard actions.

Underlining options

Word offers a variety of underlining styles, as illustrated in the table below.

Type of underlining	Effect
Words only	Underlines the words, not the spaces between
Double	A double line is used as the underline
Dotted	A dotted line is used as the underline
Thick	A thick line is used as the underline
Dash	A dashed line is used as the underline
Dot dash	An alternate dot dash line is used as the underline
Dot dot dash	A dot dot dash line is used as the underline
Wave	A wavy line is used as the underline

To choose from the different underlining options:

1. Use the **Format-Font** command.

2. In the Font dialog box, with the **Font** tab selected, open the **Underline** list box, by clicking on its associated down arrow.

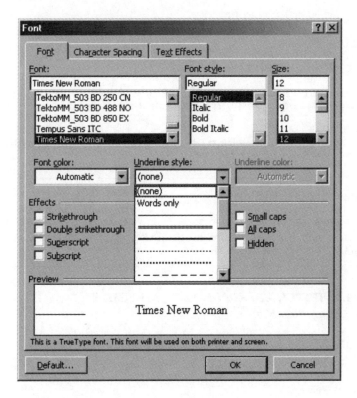

3. Select the type of underlining required.

4. Click on **OK**.

Task 1: Applying text attributes

1. Open the document *Terms of Reference* created in Unit 3 Task 1.

2. Select the heading and make it bold and underlined. (**Hint**: To select the line, point to the left-hand edge of the screen level with the heading and click.)

3. Embolden the name of the leisure centre and put the company names in italics (see illustration below). Save the document.

    Experiment by making your own selections and changing their attributes, but do not save these changes.

<u>**Terms of reference**</u>

This feasibility study looks at a complete refurbishment of the multi-gym at **Chelmer Leisure and Recreation Centre**. A wide variety of equipment could be offered in a modern fitness suite. This equipment would be a vast improvement on the existing equipment. Various equipment manufacturers have been approached and three have submitted proposals for refurbishment. This report considers each of the proposals received.

The companies from which proposals have been received are:

UNIVERSAL GYM (EUROPE) LTD
ATLANTA SPORTS INDUSTRIES LTD
PHYSIQUE TRAINING EQUIPMENT LTD

Each proposal consists of a list of equipment and plans for the fitness room, plus costings. The proposals are detailed and analysed in the report. The result of the analysis of the proposals will be a recommendation for the best option.

The report will then consider how a new fitness suite would affect the centre's usage. It will also consider ways in which the new facility should be marketed.

Task 2: Selecting text attributes

Start a new document and type in the following memo. Select the required attributes, i.e. bold, italics and underline, before keying in the text. Save as *Appointment Memo*.

---

the ***MANCHESTER METROPOLITAN UNIVERSITY***
Crewe +Alsager Faculty

MEMORANDUM
TO: R. S. Symmond
FROM: Peter Jackson
Date: 12th Feb.
Subject: <u>Final year business project</u>

When I saw you last, you suggested three possible times when we could discuss my project work, I would like to confirm that the first, *2:00pm on Monday 16th*, would suit me best and I shall see you then unless you let me know otherwise.

Using the fonts

What is a font? Word uses the word *font* to describe a typeface and its size. The typeface is the design or shape of a set of characters. Most modern inkjet and laser printers use soft fonts. These are fonts that are downloaded to the printer from the computer, such as Times New Roman, Arial and Courier New.

Word 2000 allows you to see on screen exactly what will be printed out. This is known as WYSIWYG, a mnemonic for 'What You See Is What You Get'. If you are using a laser printer or inkjet printer, the display will be identical to the final printout.

The font Courier is a fixed space font. This means that each character is the same width as every other character. This kind of typeface was common before the advent of sophisticated word processors when only simple formatting was available and text was lined up using spaces. Nowadays, most word processors, including Word, can take advantage of *proportionally spaced* fonts. With these, naturally wider characters, such as the letter m, are given more space than narrower ones, such as j.

```
Courier is a fixed space font.
```

Arial is a proportionally spaced font.

The font that you are using will appear in the font list box in the formatting toolbar. If you are using the standard default font it will be Times New Roman. On the right of this list box there is another, which contains a number. This is the point size of the characters. If you are using the default font then it will have the number 12 in it.

Choosing different fonts

Choice of font is a matter of personal taste, which should be tempered by consideration for the type of document being produced. Having chosen a particular font, it is usual to use it throughout the main body of the document. Different sizes of the chosen typeface can be used for titles, headings, headers and footers. A different font from normal could be used as an alternative to draw attention to a particular portion of the text.

The font list box in the toolbar can be opened by clicking on the down arrow to the right. The box expands to show a list of the different fonts that are available. Printer fonts have a small printer symbol next to them. Some fonts have two Ts next to them. These are known as TrueType fonts and they are the most versatile of the screen fonts because they can be varied in size in steps of one point or less.

To select a font and a size for that font:

1. Open the font list box.

2. Use the scrollbar to move through the list. There are usually more fonts than can be displayed in the box.

3. Click on the name of your chosen font.

4. Open the point size list box.

5. Use the scrollbar to move through the list of sizes. Different fonts will have different sets of sizes available.

6. Click on the size required.

The Symbol font uses the letters of the Greek alphabet and other symbols; this can be useful if you are writing a scientific report. Also there is a TrueType font called Wingdings which gives a variety of shapes and symbols, as shown below:

☞♌♏♒♈♐♑♒♓♈♋♌●○■□□□□◆♦❖◆☒☒⌘

Task 3: Applying fonts

Using *Terms of Reference*, amended in Task 1, select each company name one at a time and apply a different font. Apply different fonts to each paragraph. This creates a document that is unpleasing to read, but is a useful means of exploring the fonts available to you. Don't save the file.

Task 4: Selecting fonts

Type in the text below, selecting the fonts before keying in the text.

Questions of feasibility

Technical feasibility

Is the equipment available to support the project?

Operational feasibility

Will staff changes or training be necessary?

Economic feasibility

Will the benefits from the project outweigh the costs?

The first three lines are written using various sizes of the True Type font Arial. The next two lines are Times New Roman. The last two lines are Courier. Do not save this.

Additional font formatting

Word offers a number of additional formatting effects that can be applied through the **Format-Font** command (**Font** tab).

Effect	Appearance
Strikethrough	A line is drawn through the text
Double strikethrough	A double line is drawn through the text
Superscript	Text is positioned in a $^{\text{raised (smaller size)}}$ position
Subscript	Text is positioned in a $_{\text{lowered (smaller size)}}$ position
Shadow	Text is shadowed
Outline	Text is outlined, best used with larger font sizes
Emboss	Text is embossed
Engrave	Text is engraved
Small caps	SMALL LETTERS ARE SHOWN IN SMALLER CAPITALS
All caps	ALL TEXT IS CAPITALISED
Hidden	Hides text; options may be set to print hidden text

Other formatting effects include animation, which can be applied through the **Text Effects** tab in the Font dialog box, This kind of formatting would be appropriate for a document that is to be viewed on-line, but care should be exercised not to overdo animation effects, as the reader may find them annoying.

Controlling margins

The positions of the edges of the text on the page can be adjusted using **File-Page Setup**. In the **Margins** tab, the settings can be viewed and adjusted. There are default settings for the position of the edge of the text. For example, the default setting of the margins for A4 paper is 3.17cm in from the sides. The position of the text in relation to the top and bottom of the paper may also be adjusted.

You can also control the margins for each paragraph:

❑ The *left indent* is the position of the left edge of the text

❑ The *right indent* is the position of the right edge of the text

❑ The *first line indent* is the position of the left edge of the first line of a paragraph.

By default the left and right indents will be at the edges of the text as defined in Page Setup. The first line indent is at the same position as the left indent.

Adjusting the margins using the ruler

The ruler is displayed below other toolbars and is marked in centimetres or inches. (To change the units, select **Tools-Options**, click on the **General** tab and then select an option from the **Measurement units** box.)

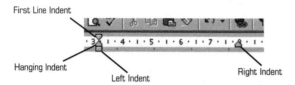

First Line Indent

Hanging Indent

Left Indent

Right Indent

On the ruler there are three triangular sliders indicating the positions of the indents. The left and right indent sliders are on the bottom of the ruler and the first line indent slider is on the top of the ruler. The box on the bottom of the ruler moves both parts of the left indent (first line indent and hanging indent).

To change	Do this
Left indent	Drag the left indent box to the required position on the ruler
Right indent	Drag the right triangle to the required position on the ruler

To set indents	Do this
First line indent	Drag the first line indent slider so that it is to the right of the left margin.
Hanging indent	Drag the hanging indent slider so it is to the right of the left margin.

Any adjustment made to the margins will affect the document at the current insertion point position and any text keyed in thereafter. Margin positions may be revised by selected the text needing revision and repositioning the indent markers.

Task 5: Controlling margins

1. With a new document open, set the left indent to 1cm and the right indent to 13cm. Type in the first paragraph of the text shown below.

2. Set the left indent to 2cm, the first line indent to 3cm and the right indent to 12cm before keying in the second paragraph.

3. The margins for the third paragraph are at left and first line 3cm, right 10cm.

4. Save this document as *Questionnaires*.

Questionnaires provide a structured and formal way in which a variety of information may be collected.

The advantages of questionnaires are that they are relatively inexpensive, they are free from interviewer distortion and if the response is anonymous, personal or controversial questions may be asked.

The disadvantages of questionnaires are that there may be a low response, questions usually have to be simple and straightforward and if they are anonymous then there is no information about the person who has answered them.

Changing existing margins

The margins of existing text can be altered by selecting that text and then adjusting the margin positions. If you alter the position of the margins when no text is selected then your alterations will only affect the paragraph that the insertion point is currently in.

Adjusting the margins using the menu

The margins may be altered more precisely using **Format-Paragraph**. Select the **Indents and Spacing** tab in the Paragraph dialog box and alter the values shown in the **Indentation** section.

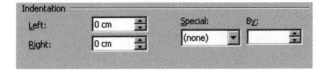

In this section there are three boxes, **Left**, **Right** and **Special**. The number in each associated box may be altered to position the margins. The **Special** list box allows the type of indenting to be chosen.

Task 6: Altering margins

Open *Terms of Reference* and change the position of the left margin of the three company name paragraphs and the indent on the first paragraph.

1. Select all three company name paragraphs and drag the left margin right by 2cm.

2. Select the first paragraph and drag the first line indent right by 1cm. Save the document.

3. Experiment by selecting other portions of the document and altering the left, right and indent margins, but do not save these changes.

Adjusting the left margin using the buttons

Word provides a quick way to adjust the left margin by means of two buttons on the formatting tool bar.

❑ The ▣ button moves the left indent in to the right by half an inch (1.27cm).

❑ The ▣ button moves the left indent out to the left by half an inch.

Task 7: A private advertisement

Create an advertisement for a student notice board. Type the following advertisement in 10-point text.

> For Sale - One pair of Ladies Ice Skates, size 6. In very good condition as only used one winter. £15 o.n.o.
>
> Contact Louise Green, Room C27, Derby Hall

To make it stand out, text attributes could be used.

> **For Sale** - One pair of ***Ladies Ice Skates, size 6***. In <u>very good condition</u> as only used one winter. £15 o.n.o.
>
> Contact **Louise Green**, Room C27, Derby Hall

Different fonts could be used to make it more eye-catching.

> **For Sale** - One pair of ***Ladies Ice Skates, size 6***. In <u>very good</u> <u>condition</u> as only used one winter. £15 o.n.o.
>
> Contact **Louise Green**, Room C27, Derby Hall

The first paragraph could have a hanging indent set, producing the following effect.

> **For Sale** - One pair of ***Ladies Ice Skates, size 6***. In <u>very good</u> <u>condition</u> as only used one winter. £15 o.n.o.
>
> Contact **Louise Green**, Room C27, Derby Hall

Formatting Paragraphs

What you will learn in this unit

This unit continues the theme of text formatting developed in Unit 4. At the end of this unit you will be able to:

❑ Create a hanging indent.

❑ Use bullets and point numbers.

❑ Change the alignment of text.

❑ Alter the spacing between lines and characters.

It is worth the effort of practising the creation of indents as this can enable you to produce documents where the text lines up correctly. The aim of text formatting is to produce a professional and pleasing document.

What you should know already

Before you start this unit, make sure you can do the following:

Skill	Covered in
Create and save a document	Unit 1
Open and edit a document	Unit 2
Select text	Unit 3
Apply fonts, control margins	Unit 4

Hanging indent

A hanging indent is where the left and indent margins are set up so that the left margin is to the right of the indent margin. Hanging indents are commonly used where a list of points is being made and the first words of a paragraph need to stand out.

Task 1: Setting a hanging indent

This task creates the example below.

1. Use a new document, type in the two lines of the heading (try to reproduce the font) and press *Enter* twice.

CHELMER LEISURE AND RECREATION CENTRE

AEROBICS OPEN DAY

Step   One of the best ways to start your fitness programme.
                  Our fitness demonstrators will be on hand to advise you
                  on a suitable fitness programme.

Cycle   Tone up those flabby thighs and strengthen those backs.
                  Our cycles simulate real cycling conditions, which can
                  be individually tailored to your fitness programme.

Row   Fancy yourself in the boat race? Try your hand at our
                  computer controlled rowing machine.

---

2. Drag the hanging indent marker to 4cm and the right indent marker to 12cm.

3. Key in the type of activity using the font Arial, bold and size 14.

4. After keying in the activity name press the *Tab* key to tab the insertion point to line up with the left margin.

5. Enter the rest of the text comprising the activity; it will wrap around onto the left margin. Use a different typeface such as Times New Roman, font size 10.

6. Press *Enter* for a new line.

7. Repeat steps 3-6 for each aerobic activity.

8. Save this document as *Open Day*.

Bullets and numbered points

To distinguish a list of points from the rest of the text it is usual to highlight them using bullets or point numbers. A bullet is a symbol at the start of each point, as shown in Task 3 below.

Hanging indents, as described above, are used when the text comprises a set of points. Word offers two buttons on the formatting toolbar that will help you to type a numbered or bulleted list.

Task 2: Numbered points

To create this example:

Five Fab Top Tips to Reduce Fat in Your Diet.

1. Fry less often. Grill, bake, nuke in the microwave or boil instead.
2. Trim visible fat off meat, don't eat the skin on chicken, skim fat off casseroles and buy lean cuts.
3. Cut down on chocolate, cakes, pastries and biscuits.
4. Use less cooking oil or fat, less salad oil, less mayonnaise and other sauces.
5. Be aware of the high fat content of some foods perceived as 'healthy' such as peanuts, avocado, polyunsaturated margarine and oils and 'low fat' spreads.

1. Start a new document, set the right indent at 12cm, key in the heading line in bold, 10-point and add a new line using *Enter*. Turn bold text off.

2. Click on the ▤ button. A number appears and the insertion point will be positioned on the left margin. Notice how the left and indent margins are set.

3. Type in the text for the point, press *Enter* and click. The next number is automatically incremented.

4. When you have finished the list press *Enter* and click on the ▤ button to stop automatic numbering and reset the indent margin. Save this document as *Five Fab Tips*.

Task 3: Bullet points

Start a new document and create the 'Findings from Market Research' list:

FINDINGS FROM MARKET RESEARCH

Information has been collated from the returned questionnaires resulting in:
- a consensus of opinion that present facilities are inadequate and that attendance is poor
- the numbers of users, particularly female, would increase if the facility was refurbished
- the majority of users are car owners, so promotion in a wider area could attract new clients
- nearly two thirds of the people surveyed had never used the existing multi-gym
- aerobic activities were popular
- entertainment, such as satellite television, would be an attraction in the new fitness suite.

1. Start a new document, set the right indent at 12cm, key in the heading line in bold, 10-point capitals and add a new line using *Enter*. Turn bold text off. Type in the first sentence and press *Enter*.

2. Click on the ⬛ button. A bullet will appear and the insertion point will be ready positioned on the left margin. Notice how the indent markers are set.

3. Key in the text for that point.

4. Make a new line, automatically creating the bullet for the next point. Repeat for each point.

5. After the last point press *Enter* and switch off the bulleting by clicking on the ⬛ button. Save this document as *Market Research*.

Customising bullets and numbers

When you click on the ⬛ or ⬛ buttons Word will apply the default numbering or bulleting to your document. You may customise this using **Format-Bullets and Numbering**. The Bullets and Numbering dialog box offers a choice of different styles of bullets under the **Bulleted** tab and different styles of numbering under the **Numbered** tab. Click on the style you want and click on **OK**.

To alter the font of a point number select the paragraph mark at the end of the point (click on the ¶ button to display them) and apply the formatting you require.

Task 4: Customising bullet points

In this task the bullets in the *Market Research* document will be modified.

1. Highlight the bulleted paragraphs in this document.

2. Choose **Format-Bullets and Numbering**.

3. Select a different bullet from those presented by clicking on it and click on **OK**.

4. Save the document.

Text alignment

Alignment is the way in which the text appears between the left and right margins. In Word there are four types of alignment: left, right, centre and full justification. Depressing the appropriate button on the formatting toolbar alters the type of alignment.

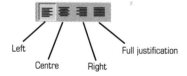

Left alignment causes the text to have a straight left margin and an uneven right margin. The uneven right margin is caused because there is a standard space between each word and each character has a specified amount of space associated with it. If a word does not fit at the end of the line then it is wrapped around onto the next line. This paragraph is written using left alignment.

Centre alignment causes each line of a paragraph to be positioned centrally between the left and right margins. If you use centre alignment while typing, the insertion point will start a new line in the centre. As the left edge of the text moves to the left the insertion point moves to the right. This type of alignment is very useful for headings, title pages, menus and posters.

Right alignment is the opposite of left alignment, so the right margin is straight and the left margin is uneven, as demonstrated in this paragraph. Right alignment is used in letters or memos where the address, date or reference number is to appear on the right-hand side of the page.

Fully justified alignment is where both the right and the left margins have straight edges. The way that this is done is by the word processor inserting extra gaps into the line so that the words line up at the right-hand edge (as in this paragraph). This type of alignment is commonly chosen for many types of document.

Task 5: Selecting alignment

1. Start a new document to create a front page for the report. Set the right indent at 12cm.

**the Manchester Metropolitan University
Crewe + Alsager Faculty**

Environment & Enterprise Project
**The Refurbishment of the Multi-Gym into a
Fitness Suite
at Chelmer Leisure and Recreation Centre
A Feasibility Study**

*By: Sarah Leveridge
Tutor: R. S. Symmond
Course: HND Business and Finance
Date: 1st February 2001*

---

2. Select Arial, 15-point text for the name of the institution.

3. For the title, select centre alignment by clicking on the appropriate icon.

4. Key in the words 'Environment & Enterprise Project' using Times New Roman, bold, italic, 15-point. Press *Enter*.

5. For the main title use Times New Roman, bold, 16-point.

6. Select right alignment.

7. Using Arial, italic, 14-point, key in the author, tutor, course and date.

8. Save this document as *Front Page*.

Line spacing

Line spacing refers to the space between the bottom of one line and the bottom of the next line. Normally text is typed in 'single spacing': i.e. line spacing is 1. Word automatically adjusts the line height to accommodate the size of the font you are using.

Choose **Format-Paragraph** to alter the line spacing in the document.

Three types of spacing that are most commonly used are:

❑ *Single*: single spacing that Word can increase depending on the size of font used.

❑ *1.5 lines*: one-and-a-half line spacing that Word can increase.

❑ *Double*: double spacing that Word can increase.

 This changes the spacing *within* the paragraph. You can also change the spacing *between* paragraphs (see Unit 6).

Task 6: Selecting line spacing

1. Start a new document to create the summary page below. Set the right indent at 12cm. Select Times New Roman, 10-point font.

2. Using **Format-Paragraph**, choose one-and-a-half spacing and key in the heading (in bold) and first paragraph.

3. Using **Format-Paragraph** again, select double spacing before keying in the final paragraph.

4. Save this document as *Summary*.

SUMMARY

Chelmer Leisure Centre is one of the facilities of Cheshire Leisure Services. The existing multi-gym facility has had little money spent on it over the past few years and has experienced a decrease in the number of users. Market research shows that there is a need for this particular facility to be updated.

Three manufacturers of fitness equipment have put forward proposals for the refurbishment of the multi-gym into a fitness suite. The proposal chosen is from Atlanta Sports Industries Ltd. The overall cost for refurbishment will be £21,000.

Character spacing

There is another form of spacing that can be used and that is spacing between characters. By choosing **Format-Font** and clicking on the **Character Spacing** tab. The **Spacing** list box may be opened to show the list of spacing choices. You can change the degree by which the text is expanded or condensed by entering a value in the **By** box.

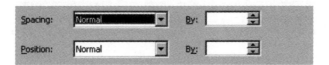

Task 7: Selecting character spacing

This task creates the following sentence:

Expanded spacing will put more space in between the letters and condensed spacing will reduce the amount of spacing between letters.

1. Start a new document. Set the right indent at 12cm. Select Times New Roman, 10-point font.

2. Choose **Format-Font** and click on the **Character Spacing** tab.

3. Open the **Spacing** box, select **Expanded** and key in the first half of the text up to the word 'and'.

4. Change to **Normal** spacing using **Format-Font** and type 'and'.

5. Change to **Condensed** spacing and key in the rest of the sentence.

Task 8: A business advertisement

The following advertisement was created using the fonts Arial and Wingdings. All the text is centre aligned.

TOP-HOLE INSURANCE
BROKERS LIMITED
**FOR ALL YOUR
INSURANCE REQUIREMENTS**

 **LOOK**

NO FURTHER
**WE CAN INSURE YOUR HOUSEHOLD
CONTENT UP TO £50,000 FOR UNDER
£1.50 PER WEEK**

MOTOR INSURANCE

OVER 25 AND NO PREVIOUS INSURANCE?

If you have held a Full Driving Licence for 4 years
with no accidents or convictions

THIRD PARTY - from only £100

FULLY COMPREHENSIVE - from only £150

Call us on (0123) 456789 *NOW!*

A variety of point sizes are used. Try point size 18 for the first two lines. Try point size 21, bold for the next two lines.

There is space above the word 'look'. Use paragraph spacing to adjust this. The hands are created using Wingdings, characters F and E, at a point size of 44. There is an easier way to find the Wingdings characters (or characters from any other font) and that is to use **Insert-Symbol** and select the symbol you require from the matrix of symbols presented. To see characters available with other fonts open the font list box and select the required font.

Try a point size of 35 for 'look', which is bold and italic.

See if you can create the rest of the advertisement. Consider the typeface, the point size, the line spacing and the character spacing of each line.

Task 9: A poster

Create the poster shown below.

Introducing the

New Generation Bodywrap System

Q.   How does it work?

A.   The Quickslim method of bodywrapping does not
depend upon fluid loss through perspiration, but on
osmotic activity reducing the inter-cellular fluid.

A course of Quickslim treatment is especially effective when
combined with a G5 treatment and a sensible diet.

See the difference for yourself!

One Wrap £38 - a 90-minute treatment

Discounts available on courses

Contact: Mary at 'The Beauty Room'

---

1. Set the left and right indents to 1cm and 13cm respectively.

2. Choose a suitably sized font and centre align the title.

3. Set a hanging indent for the question and answer. Move the hanging indent point-
    er to 2.5cm. Key in the question and answer text.

4. Put the left indent back to 1cm. Key in the paragraph of text.

5. Use centre alignment for the last section.

6. Check that you have used bold and italics where shown. Save the document as
    Poster, preview and print.

Copying formats

If you apply some formatting to a section of your text and wish to apply exactly
the same formatting to another section of your text then you can use the Format
Painter facility. To copy paragraph and character formatting:

1. Select the text that has the formatting you want to copy.

2. Click on the ✎ button in the standard toolbar.

3. Select the text to which you would like to apply the formatting.

If you wish to copy formatting to several locations then double-click on the ✎ button. Select each portion of text in turn and when you have finished click once on the ✎ button.

Task 10: Painting formats

1. Start a new document, with a right indent at 12cm. Select Times New Roman, 12-point and key in the following text but without the formatting shown.

Serif and sans serif fonts
A font is a particular design of type, which comes in a variety of styles (plain, bold, italics etc.) and a variety of sizes. Many fonts have special purposes and a typeface which works well as a header may be very hard to read if used as body text. Arial is a sans *serif* typeface, Times New Roman is a *serif* face. *Serif* are the little tails on the tips of the characters' horizontal and vertical strokes. They help to make *serif* faces look dignified, solid and unhurried.
Sans *serif* (sans means without) types are designed to be bold and easy to read, and economical with space on the paper. Sans *serif* is often used for hard information, such as instructions. It is common to have sans *serif* headlines and serif body text - *The* Guardian newspaper uses a combination of both to make up its masthead (title).
Type size
This is usually measured in points, with 72 points to the inch. But because character width, kerning (space between the letters) and leading (space between the lines) depend on how the type has been designed, type in one point size (typically 10) rarely covers the same area as the same point size in a different font. This can make layout much more complicated.

---

2. Select the text in the first heading and change it to Arial, 12-point, bold.

3. With the heading still selected, click on the ✎ button. Select the second heading and when you release the mouse button you will see the format applied.

4. Select one of the words 'serif' and make it Arial, italic.

5. While it is still selected double-click on the ✎ button. Now select each word 'serif' in turn.

6. When you have finished click once on the ✎ button.

7. Apply the formatting to 'The Guardian' and save the document as *Fonts and Size*.

Using Paragraph Styles

What you will learn in this unit

In this unit the activities continue with features that are applicable to whole paragraphs. At the end of this unit you will be able to:

❑ Change the spacing between paragraphs.

❑ Apply the same style to several paragraphs.

In Unit 5, paragraph indents were investigated. This unit considers the spacing between paragraphs. Using styles allows you to be consistent in your work in terms of the format of headings and sub-headings and the body of your text.

What you need

To complete this unit you will need:

❑ The document file *Questionnaires* created in Unit 4

❑ The document file *Front Page* created in Unit 5

Paragraph formatting

In many documents, paragraphs have space between them. Instead of pressing *Enter* to create a blank line between paragraphs Word allows you to define the amount of space before and after a paragraph. Use **Format-Paragraph** to display the Paragraph dialog box with the **Indents and Spacing** tab selected. In the spacing section the values in the **Before** and **After** boxes can be adjusted. Spacing is altered in increments of 6 points, which can be considered to be half a line (though you can type in any other value). Note that if you have space after a paragraph and the following paragraph has space before it then the space between the paragraphs will not necessarily be the sum of the before and after spacing.

Other paragraphs may require different spacing, for example headings or tables, and these can be easily adjusted from the Paragraph dialog box.

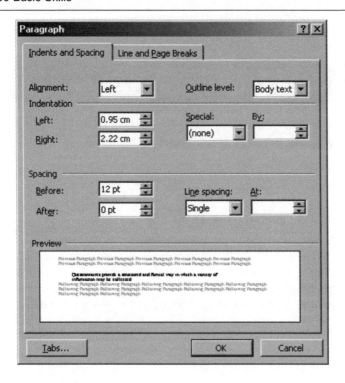

Task 1: Controlling space between paragraphs

This task experiments with altering the spacing between paragraphs. Open the document *Questionnaires*.

1. If you have blank lines in between paragraphs, remove them. Click on the ¶ button to show the paragraph marks.

2. Position the insertion point in the first paragraph.

3. Choose **Format-Paragraph** and select the **Indents and Spacing** tab. Set the spacing **After** to 12 points (one line).

4. Position the insertion point in the second paragraph.

5. Choose **Format-Paragraph** and set the spacing **After** to 24 points (two lines).

6. Position the insertion point in the third paragraph.

7. Choose **Format-Paragraph** and set the spacing **Before** to 24 points (two lines).

8. Save and print this document.

9. Experiment with setting the line spacing before and after the paragraphs in this document.

Using styles

A *style* is the name applied to the 'look' of the text in a document. The look of the text depends upon the formatting instructions that have been applied to it. A heading is usually made to look different from the body of the text, i.e. it has a different style. In a document there may be different levels of headings, for example chapter or section headings, and within these are sub-headings. Word has the facility for different styles to be created and stored under different names. Different styles can be used for different headings.

Various formatting may be applied to create a style:

1. Character formatting such as:

    ❑ Typeface

    ❑ Size

    ❑ Bold, italics or underlining

    ❑ Special effects such as shadow or outline

2. Paragraph formatting such as:

    ❑ Alignment

    ❑ Spacing

    ❑ Margins

    ❑ Pagination

3. Layout formatting such as:

    ❑ Tabs

    ❑ Bullets and numbering

    ❑ Borders and shading

4. Language formatting. If text is written in a different language then Word will know to use the appropriate dictionary (if available) when spell checking.

Selecting a style

Word comes with some predefined styles and these can be listed by opening the style list box on the formatting tool bar.

To select a style:

1. Position the insertion point, either to key in some new text or in an existing paragraph. If you wish to alter the style of a portion of the document which is more than one paragraph long, then select the required portion.

2. Open the Style list box and highlight the required style.

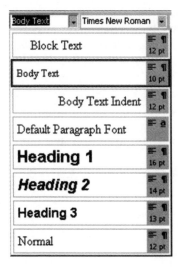

3. Either key in text which will have the selected style, or the chosen paragraph or portion will be changed into the new style.

To see the definition of a style, position the insertion point in some text that uses the style, say Normal, and choose **Format-Style**. In the Style dialog box a description of the style is given.

Styles may be used as the document is being keyed in or they can be applied after the text has been keyed in. The real advantage in using styles is in being able to define custom styles. Should an alteration in the style be desirable then by changing the definition of the style, all parts of the document that use that style will be altered accordingly. This makes it easier to produce consistent documents.

Defining a custom style

New styles can be defined, or existing ones modified, using **Format-Style**. To define the style for the main body of the text in the document:

1. Position the insertion point in a paragraph that is to take the main body style, or position it on a new line.

2. Use **Format-Style** to display the Style dialog box.

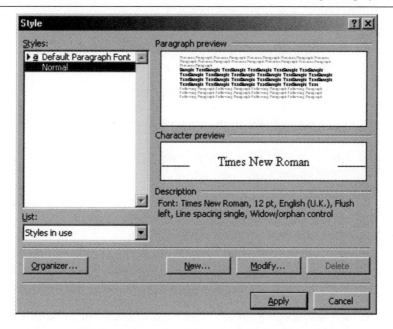

3. Click on the **New** button and the New Style dialog box appears. In the **Name** box type in the name for the new style, e.g. *Text Body*.

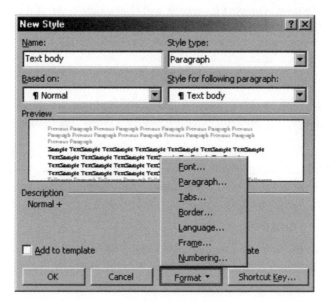

4. Select the appropriate formatting by clicking on the **Format** button and choosing from the list:

❑ **Font** produces the Font dialog box (see Unit 4).

❑ **Paragraph** produces the Paragraph dialog box (see Unit 4).

❑ **Tabs** produces the Tabs dialog box (see Unit 7).

❏ **Border** produces the Borders and Shading dialog box (see Unit 18).

❏ **Language** produces the Language dialog box (see Unit 13).

❏ **Frame** produces the Frame dialog box (see Unit 18).

❏ **Numbering** produces the Bullets and Numbering dialog box (see Unit 5).

5. Make required choices from these dialog boxes.

6. Choose the **Style for following paragraph** from the list box. In this case it would be *Text Body*. Click on **OK**.

7. When the style is defined click on **Apply**. The defined style name will be available through the style list box.

At the top of the dialog box there are two list boxes, a **Based on** box and a **Style for following paragraph** box. By basing your custom styles on one particular style formatting changes can be made easier. If all the styles are based on a style that has a Times New Roman font and a decision is made to change to Arial then by altering the font upon which the others are all based will cause them to be altered (unless they have specific character formatting applied).

The **Style for following paragraph** list box defines the style that is to follow the one being used. The next paragraph will take on the style of the 'next style'. For the *Text Body* style the next style should be *Text Body* as the most likely paragraph to follow a paragraph of straight text is another paragraph using the same format. If the style is a heading style, e.g. *Heading 1*, then it is most likely that a text body paragraph will follow, so for *Heading 1* the next style should also be *Text Body*.

Note that heading styles (there are 9, *Heading 1* to *Heading 9*) should only be used for headings. If a table of contents is required Word uses headings to generate it.

It is worth the extra effort in designing various styles to give your work a professional look. Do not use lots of different fonts; the best effects are achieved with one font used in different sizes rather than with a variety of text attributes.

Task 2: Defining and using styles

For this task open the document file *Front Page*. Formatting that has been previously set up can be defined as a style. Four styles are to be defined for this title page.

1. First position the insertion point in the first line of the title page.

2. Use **Format-Style**, click on **New** and in the **Name** box type in the name *Title1*.

3. Click on **OK** and then on the **Apply** button.

4. Select the second line, open the style list box and select *Title1*. Nothing appears to happen except that the style of *Title1* has been applied to that paragraph.

5. Position the insertion point in the author name. As above, create a style called *Title4*.

6. Apply this style to the last four lines of the page. You may need to click on the **Format** button in the Style dialog box and choose **Paragraph** to remove spacing before/after a paragraph.

7. In a similar manner define and apply suitable styles, *Title2* and *Title3*, to the second and third portions of the page. (**Hint**: keep paragraph spacing to zero; add spacing to the first line of a portion after the styles have been defined.)

8. Save the document as *Front Page*.

Task 3: Modifying a style

You may change your mind about the styles that you have chosen and wish to make changes.

Using the file *Front Page* make changes to the styles created in Task 2.

1. Position the insertion point in text that has the style *Title1* applied to it.

2. Choose **Format-Style** and click on **Modify**. Click on **Format**, choose **Font** and select a different font. Click on **OK**.

3. Click on **OK** in the **Modify Style** dialog box and click on **Apply**. All text throughout the document defined with this style will take on these new properties.

4. Experiment with the other styles. Changes to their fonts, sizes, margins and alignment can be made. If you prefer the styles you have chosen, save the document.

Using Tabs

What you will learn in this unit

This unit focuses on activities associated with the creation of tables of text and numbers using tab stops. At the end of this unit you will be able to:

❏ Use and change default tab stops to set up a simple table.

❏ Set custom tab stops.

❏ Use different types of tab stops.

❏ Insert tab stops in an existing document.

Familiarity with such operations will allow you to construct documents such as tables of numbers or text, curriculum vitae, questionnaires and forms. Unit 16 explores a further way of setting up such tables.

Important note – using the spacebar

It is frequently necessary to be able to present text or numbers as lists in columns. If you are accustomed to using a typewriter you may have used the *spacebar* to align text. **Do not** use the *spacebar* to format or align text with a word processor. The *spacebar* should only be used to insert a space between words. If you attempt to use the *spacebar* to align text in columns, this will impede later formatting and although columns may appear aligned on the screen they will not be aligned when printed out. Modern printers use proportionally-spaced fonts where different letters are allocated different amounts of space. It is essential to use the facilities described in this and Unit 16 in order to produce effective tables.

Default tab stops

The simplest way to create text that is lined up in columns is to use tab stops. If you inspect the ruler (if the ruler is not displayed then display it by selecting **View-Ruler**), you will see that Word provides default left tab stops at approximately every half inch. Tabs are shown as small vertical lines along the bottom of the ruler. Text can be aligned at these tab stops simply by pressing the *Tab* key to move to the next tab stop position.

The default tab stops can be changed by choosing **Format-Tabs**, making appropriate changes in the **Default Tab Stops** box and then clicking on **OK**.

Task 1: Using default tab stops

With a new document open:

1. Type in the following text, using Courier New 12-point, working one line at a time and using the *Tab* key to move between one column and the next.

```
Opening Times

Health Suite

Monday     9.00am - 9.00pm      Ladies Only

Tuesday    9.00am - 9.00pm      Mixed

Wednesday 9.30am - 9.00pm       Mixed

Thursday   9.00am - 1.00pm      Ladies Only

           1.00pm - 9.00pm      Mixed

Friday     9.00am - 9.00pm      Men Only

Saturday   9.00am - 1.00pm      Men Only

           1.00pm - 5.00pm      Mixed

Sunday     9.00am - 5.00pm      Mixed
```

2. Press the *Enter* key to move onto a new line.

3. Finally format the headings as shown in the example.

Now change the default tab stops so that the final column is further away from the times, by choosing **Format-Tabs** and using the **Default Tab Stops** box to increase the distance between the default tab stops to 1.5cm. Notice the effect on your document. Note that if you set the distance between default tab stops to 2cm the document loses its columnar appearance. This is because some words (e.g.

Wednesday) are longer than others and the longer words obscure a tab stop whereas the shorter ones don't. To avoid this it is better to set custom tab stops on the ruler, as will be seen in the next section. Save this document as *Health Suite Times*.

Types of tab stop

There are four types of tab stop: left, centre, right and decimal. Each of these may be set by clicking on the **Tab** button at the left-hand side of the ruler, which in the default mode is shown as a left tab . Clicking on this button causes it to cycle through the different tab types.

Button	Tab type	Tab function
	*Left*	Text is aligned with its left edge on the tab stops; this is the usual typewriter type of tab and is the default. This is useful for aligning columns of words.
	*Centre*	Text is centred beneath the tab stop. This can be useful in advertisements and other documents where you wish to display a text list.
	*Right*	Text is aligned with its right edge under the tab stop. This is useful for numbers that do not contain a decimal point and for text that must be aligned in a column against, say, the right margin.
	*Decimal*	Numbers are aligned with the decimal point beneath the tab stop. Clearly useful for numbers, particularly money.

Setting tab stops with the ruler and the mouse

It is easiest in the first instance if you insert tab stops before creating text, rather than try to add them later, although this is perfectly possible once you are confident with the use of tab stops.

To add a tab stop:

1. Select the paragraphs to which you want to add tab stops, or position the insertion point where you want the formatting with tab stops to start as you type the document.

2. Click on the **Tab** button until it displays the tab type that you wish to use, i.e. left, right, centre or decimal.

3. Point to where you wish to place the tab on the ruler and click to place a tab stop at that point. The tab should appear on the ruler as a tiny version of the tab symbol on the button.

This procedure can be repeated to add other tab stops.

Ruler without custom tab stops; the default tabs can just be seen on the lower part of the ruler at half inch intervals.

Ruler showing custom tabs. There is a left tab at approximately 1.5cm, a centre tab at 4.5cm, a right tab at 7.5cm and a decimal tab at 11.5cm.

Clearing custom tab stops with the ruler

To clear custom tab stops:

1. Select the paragraph that contains the tab stops to be cleared.

2. On the ruler click on the tab stop that you want to remove, then drag it out of the ruler.

Customising tab stops with the Tabs command

The **Tabs** command offers a further way of controlling various aspects of tab stops. With the appropriate paragraph selected, choose **Format-Tabs**. This displays the Tabs dialog box.

This box allows you to change the format of existing tabs or to add any new tabs. Formatting will be applied to the tab displayed in the box at the top of the **Tab stop position** box. You can enter a new tab position in this box, or display an existing tab by selecting it from further down the **Tab stop position** box. For each tab, it is possible to set its alignment and leader. A leader is a series of characters that appear before the text at the tab stop, such as a series of dots. After specifying these characteristics, click on the **Set** button. The position of the default stops may be adjusted; stops may be cleared using the **Clear** or **Clear All** buttons. Exit with **OK** to accept the new settings.

Task 2: Setting tab stops

1. Open the *Health Suite Times* document that you created in Task 1 and move the pointer to the end of the existing text. You will add the following text:

Health Suite Passcards

Gold Passcard. Use of all our facilities including the Health Suite, Fitness Suite, Pool and Oasis.

3 Month	Gold Pass	£85.00
6 Month	Gold Pass	£150.00
12 Month	Gold Pass	£275.00

This uses the following tabs:

❏ A left tab at approximately 2.5cm (1.00")

❏ A centre tab at 6.5cm (2.50")

❏ A right tab at 10.25cm (4.00")

2. Click on the **Tab** button on the ruler and choose the left tab type.

3. Point to where you wish to place the tab on the ruler and click to place a tab stop at that point.

4. Repeat for the other two tabs.

5. Type in the text, using the *Tab* key to move between tab stops.

6. Now reformat the tabs. Select the text that you have just entered and use the **Format-Tabs** command to display the Tabs dialog box.

7. Select the first tab, change its alignment to **Right** and introduce a leader with ...

8. Click on **Set**, then **OK**. Note the effect that this has on your document.

9. Save the document.

Task 3: Inserting tabs in an existing document

This task asks you to insert a paragraph with new tabs in the middle of a document. Newcomers to word processing often have difficulty with this, so it is worth practising.

With the document called *Health Suite Times* open:

1. Move the insertion point to a position between the two pieces of text that you entered for Tasks 1 and 2.

2. Open up some space by pressing *Enter*.

3. Move the insertion point back to the top of this space.

4. Prepare to insert the following table.

```
Fitness Suite

Monday        8.00am - 8. 00pm

              8.00pm - 9. 00pm      Super Circuit

Tuesday       9.00am - 9. 00pm

Wednesday     9.30am - 8. 00pm

              8.00am - 9. 00pm      Super Circuit

Thursday      9.00am - 9. 00pm

Friday        9.00am - 9. 00pm

Saturday      9.00am - 5. 00pm

Sunday        9.00am - 5. 00pm
```

5. Set a centre tab at approximately 3.5cm (1.4") and a left tab at 8.25cm (3.2") using the ruler.

6. Enter text using the *Tab* key to move between stops.

7. Now move up and down the document and examine the different tab stops as they are applied to different parts of the document.

8. Save the document and close it.

Using Columns

What you will learn in this unit

This unit introduces the use of columns and associated formatting options that might help you to produce a document such as a newsletter. At the end of this unit you will be able to:

❏   Create a document that uses columns.

This unit focuses on the creation of relatively short documents such as newsletters that integrate text, formatted in various ways, with graphics and images. In the design of such documents there is a significant emphasis on the page layout, so it is useful to work in Page Layout view, and to remember to make full use of Print Preview before printing the document.

Word is primarily suitable for the design of simply formatted newsletters. It does, however, offer a wide range of desktop publishing features, and you will need to evaluate whether it is appropriate for any more significant applications that you might have, or whether to opt for a desktop publishing package.

Working with columns

Word allows you to produce two types of columns. The first kind of column is the snaking column, in which text flows from the bottom of one column to the top of the next, as in newspaper columns. Unit 16 introduces columns in tables, which are parallel columns.

Document views

When entering text you will probably have used Normal view most of the time. This is easy for fast text entry, but does not display columns side by side.

Page Layout view is preferable when using columns, as it shows columns side by side with items such as graphics in the correct location. It is useful for editing, manually inserting column breaks, and adjusting column width. You can zoom in or out.

Print Preview shows the overall page layout, just as the document will be printed. You can edit text, and make adjustments to margins and page breaks.

Creating multiple column layout

To create a multiple column layout:

1. Choose **View-Page Layout**.

2. Click in the section to be formatted.

3. Use **Format-Columns**.

4. Specify the number of columns: for example, 2.

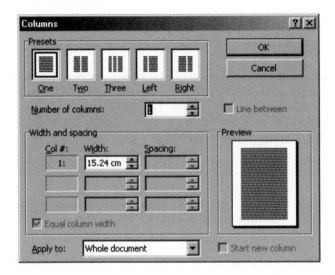

5. In the **Apply To** box, select the portion of the document that you want to format.

6. Click on **OK**.

Alternatively:

1. Choose **View-Page Layout**.

2. Click in the section to be formatted.

3. Click on the ▦ button on the toolbar.

4. Drag to the right to select the number of columns that you want.

When you release the mouse button, Word formats the section that contains the insertion point.

You can also use the **Format-Columns** command to:

❑ Change the space between columns, through the **Width and spacing** section.

❑ Add a vertical line between columns, through the **Line between** box.

❑ Format the current section to start in a new column through the **Start new column** box.

You can change the number of columns in all or part of a document. To change the number of columns on part of a document, make that part a separate section by inserting a section break (see Unit 11). Within each section Word automatically adjusts the width of the columns. Word adjusts the space between columns to create equal amounts of space. You can customise this for unequal spacing through the **Width and spacing** section.

Note: Word stores the formatting instructions for a section in the section mark. If you delete a section mark, any text in the section assumes the format of the text below it. If you delete a section break accidentally, do not forget your old friend Edit-Undo.

Task 1: Setting up a newsletter

In this task we wish to set up the basic format for the newsletter. First you can add the heading and then insert the columns.

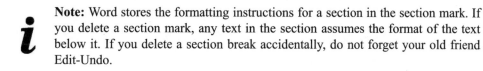

Chelmer Leisure and Recreation Centre

Fitness News

The Benefits of Exercise

Whallop! It hits you!! When your most energetic event over the last few weeks was getting up to change the TV channel because the remote control wasn't working, you suddenly realise that physical exertion can be quite unpleasant!

But fear not! After only a short spell at an activity class the benefits will start to show. You can expect an increase in stamina (those stairs won't seem so steep anymore), strengthening and toning of your once invisible muscles, and an increase in the range of movement of those aching joints.

Open a new document. Check that the correct printer is selected using **File-Print**. Also choose the correct page size (A4) using **File-Page Setup**. Choose **View-Page Layout**. Type 'Chelmer Leisure and Recreation Centre' across the top of the document, press *Enter* and type 'Fitness News'. Press *Enter* to make some space in the document below the text.

Next format this heading, as follows:

1.   Apply centre justification.

2.   Select a typeface and size that cause the first line to fill the width of the page.

3.   Format the text as bold.

4.   Create some space above and beneath the text. (**Hint**: use spacing **Before** for the first line of the title and spacing **After** for the second line.)

5.   Next we wish to create two columns.

6.   Place the insertion point below the heading.

7.   Choose **Format-Columns**.

8.   Select the number of columns below the heading: i.e. **Two**.

9.   Select **This point forward** in the **Apply To** box.

10. Check the **Line between** check box.

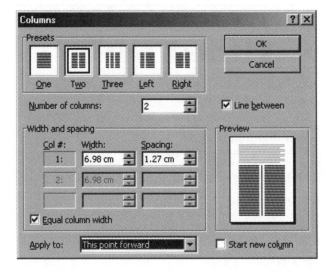

11. Click on **OK**. Word places a section break between the heading and the multiple columns. (This break is not visible in Page Layout view. See Unit 11 for information on sections.)

12. Finally, save this document, using **File-Save**, as *News1*.

Task 2: Putting text into columns

With the document *News1* open, start to enter the following text at the top of the first column. Format the heading appropriately. Notice that the text is formatted into the first column.

The Benefits of Exercise

Whallop! It hits you!! When your most energetic event over the last few weeks was getting up to change the TV channel because the remote control wasn't working, you suddenly realise that physical exertion can be quite unpleasant!

But fear not! After only a short spell at an activity class the benefits will start to show. You can expect an increase in stamina (those stairs won't seem so steep anymore), strengthening and toning of your once invisible muscles, and an increase in the range of movement of those aching joints.

Save the document as *News1*.

Using AutoFormat Options

What you will learn in this unit

When you are creating a document the best way to achieve a professional effect is to use paragraph styles. Styles enable you to be consistent throughout the document for example, in your use of headings. If you are fairly new to using Word then applying styles may seem a little difficult. To help overcome this difficulty Word has an AutoFormatting facility which will apply an attractive format to your text by applying a built-in style.

As you add text to the document then AutoFormat can be applied to this to maintain the consistency of your document. If you have already applied some formatting to the document the AutoFormat facility can uniformly apply this to the rest of the document. At the end of this unit you will be able to:

❏ Choose AutoFormat options.

❏ AutoFormat simple documents.

❏ Review AutoFormatting changes.

What you need

To complete this unit you will need:

❏ The document file *Centre Introduction* created in Unit 3

❏ The document file *Market Research* created in Unit 5

Setting up AutoFormat

Before using AutoFormat you should review the AutoFormat settings. There are two categories, **AutoFormat** and **AutoFormat As You Type**. To display the AutoFormat settings use **Tools-AutoCorrect** and click on the **AutoFormat** tab.

This dialog box allows you to set rules that Word's AutoFormatting facility will follow.

Apply section	
Headings	Automatically applies *Heading 1* to *Heading 9* styles to headings; for example, the headings in outlines or legal documents.

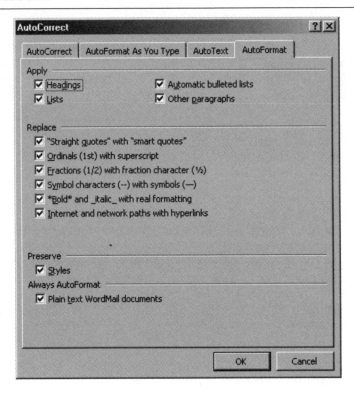

Lists

Automatically applies list and bullet styles to numbered, bulleted and multi-level lists. Word removes any manually inserted numbers or bullets before automatically applying the built-in list or bullet styles.

Automatic bulleted lists   Automatically adds bullets to a list.

Other paragraphs

Automatically applies paragraph styles other than the styles for headings and lists, such as the *Body Text* style.

Replace section

Straight quotes with smart quotes	Changes straight quotation marks (" " and ' ') to smart (curly) quotation marks (" " and ' ')
Ordinals (1st) with superscript	Automatically changes normal typing into superscript where it is being used for an ordinal e.g. 9th.
Fractions (1/2) with fraction character (½)	Converts ordinary typing (e.g. 1/4) to fraction symbols; works for ½ and ¼.
Symbol characters (--) with (–) symbols	Replaces characters used in place of symbols with symbols that may not be on your keyboard but that your printer can print. For example, you can replace

(TM) with the trademark symbol, ™. Word can display and print symbols if you have installed a screen font and a printer font that contain those symbols. If you have only the printer font, the symbols will be printed properly but may not appear correctly on the screen.

Bold and _underline_ with real formatting	Removes the * and _ symbols often used in e-mail and emboldens or italicises the text.
Internet and network paths with hyperlinks	Creates a hyperlink when a URL address (Internet path) is keyed in.

Preserve section

Styles	Retains existing styles when Word automatically formats the document.

Always AutoFormat section

Plain text WordMail documents	Applies AutoFormatting to documents received by WordMail.

To display the AutoFormat As You Type settings use **Tools-AutoCorrect** and click on the **AutoForrnat As You Type** tab. Many of the options that can be set for AutoFormat can be set for AutoFormat As You Type. Some of the typing aids you may set are listed in the following table.

Apply as you type section

Borders	If you type three or more hyphens (-), underscore characters (_) or equals signs (=) and press _Enter_ Word will replace them with the thin, thick or double line bottom border style.
Tables	If you type a combination of plus signs and hyphens (+———+———+————+) Word will convert them to a table with the columns indicated by the plus signs.
Automatic bulleted lists	If you type an asterisk (*), a lower case o, a greater than symbol (>) or a hyphen (-) followed by a space or a tab and then some text, Word will convert this to a bulleted list.
Automatic numbered lists	This is similar to bulleted lists except that if you type a number followed by a tab and then some text Word will convert the text to a numbered list.

The options in the **Replace as you type** section are as for AutoFormat.

Automatically as you type section

Format beginning of list item like the one before it	If the point, first word or first phase is formatted in a different way from the following text, to make it stand out, then Word applies this formatting to subsequent points.
Define styles based on your formatting	If you change the formatting of text to which a style has been applied, the style (and all text formatted with that style) is modified accordingly.

Using the AutoFormat command

By default, the AutoFormat command applies a style to each paragraph currently formatted with the *Normal* or *Body Text* styles. Also by default, Word preserves any styles, such as list or heading styles, you have previously applied to the document.

If you want Word to ignore previously applied styles and format your document with appropriately chosen styles, choose **Tools-AutoCorrect**, and in the **AutoFormat** tab, clear the **Styles** check box in the **Preserve** section. The next time you use the AutoFormat command, Word will apply the built-in styles.

To format text automatically:

1. To format the entire document, position the insertion point anywhere in the document. To format a selection, select the text you want to format.

2. Choose **Format-AutoFormat**. Select the **AutoFormat now** option. Choose *General document* as a guide for formatting. Word reformats the document analysing the text and applying styles from the attached template. Word formats the document or selected text according to the options you selected on the AutoFormat section of the Options dialog box (**Tools** menu). If you do not want to preserve the new formatting then you may use **Edit-Undo** to return to the original formatting.

To format text and then review the changes:

1. Select the document or part of document that you want to reformat. Choose **Format-AutoFormat** and select the **AutoFormat and review each change** option.

2. Choose **General document** as a guide for formatting.

3. Word then displays the AutoFormat dialog box. Click on **Accept All** to accept all the changes, **Reject All** to reject all the changes, **Review Changes** to accept some changes and reject others, and **Style Gallery** to select a different template.

4. Choosing **Review Changes** displays the Review AutoFormat Changes dialog box. Use the **Find** buttons to move through the document and review the formatting changes. If the dialog box needs moving, drag it by its title bar.

5. Word describes the selected change in the Review AutoFormat Changes dialog box. To make alterations to styles use the style list box on the formatting toolbar. Do any of the following:

To	Do this
Undo the displayed change	Choose the **Reject** button
Undo the last rejected change	Choose the **Undo** button
Display the document as it will appear if you accept all remaining changes	Choose the **Hide Marks** button
Redisplay the change markings	Choose the **Show Marks** button

6. When you have finished, click on **Cancel** and then click on **Accept All**.

7. If you decide to undo all changes after you've chosen the **Accept All** button to close the AutoFormat dialog box, click the **Undo** button on the standard tool-bar.

Note: The AutoFormat command does not format Word tables. The automatic formatting of tables, using the **Table-Table AutoFormat** command, is discussed in Unit 16.

Task 1: Style formatting

In this task the AutoFormat command will be used to apply a heading style and to adjust spacing between paragraphs. Create the text used in Unit 3 Task 3 (*Centre Introduction*) without any formatting and use a blank line between paragraphs.

1. Choose **Format-AutoFormat**.

2. Word displays a dialog box asking you to confirm that you want to format the document. Select the **AutoFormat now** option and the *General document* style, and click on **OK**. Word analyses the text and applies styles from the attached template.

INTRODUCTION

The Chelmer Leisure and Recreation Centre is at present a very basic gym. It is used by people from a wide range of socio-economic backgrounds. The majority of people using the centre come from the surrounding catchment area.

It is proposed to apply for Local Council funding for refurbishing the present multi-gym facility into a fitness suite. In recent years little money has been spent on the multi-gym. This has resulted in a decrease in the number of users. Present users of the multi-gym are weightlifters most of whom are male.

The fitness centre offers a wide range of activities. The centre is also an extremely popular venue for aerobics, step classes, keep fit and popmobility. These classes are responsible for attracting a large number of female users to the centre, who, in the event of refurbishment of the multi-gym, would be a large target group. The aerobic-based activities account for nearly half of the total number of users of the centre. It is hoped that with the introduction of a fitness suite, those existing users will also use the new facility.

---

3. Note the styles that have been applied: *Heading 1* for the heading and *Body Text* for the rest of the text. Select one of these paragraphs and use **Format-Style** to investigate the effect of AutoFormat. What paragraph spacing has Word applied? (Do not save this file.)

Task 2: Correcting 'bad' word processing using AutoFormat

This task examines the effect that AutoFormat has on 'bad' word processing, i.e. text that has a new line at the end of each line and the use of spaces to line up columns. Create the text used in the previous task but do not use word wrap; force each new line by pressing *Enter*.

1. Choose **Format-AutoFormat**. Select the **AutoFormat now** option and *General document* style, and click on **OK** to AutoFormat the document.

2. As before, styles will have been applied and the paragraph marks at the end of each line removed. (Do not save this file.)

Task 3: Bullet and numbered list formatting as you type

First check that the options **Automatic bulleted lists** and **Automatic numbered lists** in the **AutoFormat As You Type** section of the AutoCorrect dialog box are ticked.

1. Key in the text of *Market Research* (created in Unit 5).

2. When you reach the first bulleted point type an asterisk, a space and the rest of the sentence.

3. When you press *Enter* Word automatically converts your typing into a bulleted list. You can continue to enter the rest of the points. Note that you may reject this type of change in circumstances where it is inappropriate, either via the Office Assistant or using **Undo**.

Information has been collated from the returned questionnaires resulting in:

*   a consensus of opinion that present facilities are inadequate and that attendance is poor
*   the numbers of users, particularly female, would increase if the facility was refurbished
*   the majority of users are car owners, so promotion in a wider area could attract new clients
*   nearly two thirds of the people surveyed had never used the existing multi-gym
*   aerobic activities were popular
*   entertainment, such as satellite television, would be an attraction in the new fitness suite.

Repeat this task for the numbered list *Five Fab Tips* (also created in Unit 5). For the first point type the number, a space and the text for the point. What happens when you press *Enter*? (Do not save this file.)

Task 4: Reviewing changes

The document used for this task is shown below. Key it in and save it as *Dialog Boxes*.

1. Load the document *Dialog Boxes*. Choose **Format-AutoFormat**, select the **AutoFormat and review each change** option and *General document* formatting. Click on **OK**.

2. When the AutoFormatting is complete click on **Review Changes**.

THE DIALOG BOXES

Windows applications use dialog boxes to request information from you and to output information that is not a part of the normal data display. Another type of box, the message box, is used when displaying error messages and warnings to the user. If a menu item is followed by three periods (...), that means it displays a dialog box. Dialog boxes contain one or more special features, or controls. Dialog boxes can support any of five types of controls, these are command buttons, option buttons, check boxes, list boxes and text boxes.

Command button

A command button looks like a labelled button. Examples include the OK and Cancel buttons. If the label ends with a period, clicking the button will activate another dialog box. If the button contains an underlined letter, it can be activated from the keyboard using the combination ALT-letter.

Option buttons

A round button (or "radio button") that permits you to select only one item from a group. The button is displayed as a small circle. You can select the desired button with a mouse or use the direction keys and the spacebar.

Check box

A toggle that turns a feature or state either on or off. The toggle is displayed as a small square which is either blank or has a tick in it. It can be toggled by pointing and clicking with the mouse or pressing the spacebar.

List box

A box showing multiple choices, such as the Look in list box on the Open dialog box. With a list box, use the mouse or direction keys to highlight your selection and then double-click, or press Enter, or click the OK button. You can also press any letter to move the highlight to the first selection starting with the letter. For long lists, the control has a vertical scroll bar at the right that simplifies movement to the item required. In small dialog boxes with long lists, a drop-down list box is used to conserve space. The list is opened from a single line list box with an arrow in a square box at the right. Click on this arrow to open the box. Then select with a mouse, From the keyboard, hold down the ALT key and then press the down arrow to open the box, select the option with the direction keys and press ALT+down arrow again. Text box

A box for entering text data. When it is selected, an insertion point appears in the box. You can enter or edit the text before pressing Enter or clicking on OK.

You can use either the mouse or keyboard to move about in a dialog box and choose controls. The dialog box displays default settings. To select a control with a mouse, click it. To select a control with the keyboard, use TAB or SHIFT+TAB to move to the desired control. After the control is selected, set it using one of the ways described above. Close the box by clicking on OK to keep changes or Cancel if you change your mind and wish to leave things as they were.

Note: Most dialog boxes can't be resized.

3. Click on the ➜ **Find** button and note in the description box that the first change was the application of the *Heading 1* style.

4. Click on ➜ **Find** and each time note the description of the change.

5. Using the **Find** buttons (to move forwards and backwards through the changes) find the first instance of where a straight quote was replaced by smart quotes and click on **Reject**.

6. Find all other instances of this change and reject them.

7. Click on **Cancel** and **Accept All**.

8. Alter the *Body Text* style to be 12-point. Select the first paragraph and change its point size to 12. Click on *Body Text* in the **Style** box and choose to redefine the style. This change should affect all paragraphs with the style *Body Text*.

9. Save.

Formatting Pages

What you will learn in this unit

In this unit the tasks concentrate on word-processing features that are applicable to documents of more than one page. If the work being produced is for assessment it is often in the form of a report and may be several pages long. At the end of this unit you will he able to:

❑ Insert page breaks.

❑ Number pages.

❑ Add headers and footers.

❑ Add footnotes and endnotes.

For most long documents it is useful to know how to add headers, footers and page numbers and to be able to control page breaks.

You may be working on a report and have information in several files. These files can be combined into one file so that, for example, appropriate headers and footers and page numbers may be added. In the following example, a large document will be created from smaller documents created in previous tasks.

What you need

To complete this unit you will need:

❑ The document file *Front Page* created in Unit 5 and amended in Unit 6

❑ The document file *Terms of Reference* created in Unit 3 and amended in Unit 4

❑ The document file *Centre Introduction* created in Unit 3

❑ The document file *Centre Usage* created in Unit 3

❑ The document file *Questionnaires* created in Unit 4 and amended in Unit 6

❑ The document file *Market Research* created in Unit 5

❑ The document file *Summary* created in Unit 5

Task 1: Combining smaller documents into a larger one

Documents needed for this task are *Front Page*, *Terms of Reference*, *Centre Introduction*, *Centre Usage*, *Questionnaires*, *Market Research* and *Summary*.

1. Start a new document file and, using **File-Save As**, save this as *Report*.

2. Choose **Insert-File** and the File dialog box appears.

3. From the list of files select the file *Front Page* and click on **OK**.

4. Move to the end of the document.

5. Repeat steps 2–4 to insert each of the document files *Terms of Reference*, *Centre Introduction*, *Centre Usage*, *Questionnaires*, *Market Research* and *Summary*.

6. Tidy up the text and paragraph formatting, to give a consistent look and feel to the document.

7. Save this file using **File-Save**.

Pagination and page numbering

As the document being created gets larger Word automatically inserts a page break at the end of each page. Automatic page breaks are called *soft breaks* and are shown in Normal view as a dotted line. As the document is edited and revised Word repositions the page breaks accordingly. This is known as *repagination*. Repagination occurs whenever you pause during keying. To alter the way in which page breaks occur then manual or *hard* breaks can be inserted.

Adding or removing page breaks

To add a page break, first position the insertion point at the place where the page break is to occur, then do one of the following:

❏ Use **Insert-Break** and select **Page break** from the Break dialog box.

❏ Use the keyboard shortcut, pressing *Ctrl/Enter* simultaneously.

In Normal view a dotted line appears at the point of the page break. In a hard break the words *Page Break* appear in the middle of the line.

A hard page break may be selected in the same way as a line of text is selected: i.e. by positioning the mouse pointer in the left edge of the screen, level with the page break, and clicking. Once selected, the page break can be removed. It is not possible to remove soft page breaks; these can be controlled either by inserting hard page breaks or with paragraph formatting. If possible it is best to avoid hard page breaks in a long document as they need to be revised manually whenever the document is revised.

Task 2: Page breaks

1. Open the file *Report* created in Task 1 to insert appropriate page breaks.

2. Position the cursor at the start of 'Terms of Reference' and press *Ctrl/Enter*. This should insert a hard break after the title page. The body of the report should start on the next page.

3. Repeat this process to put a page break before each heading. You may try adjusting the spacing on the title page to spread out the titles.

4. Use **File-Print Preview** to see how the document looks. Save this document as *Report*.

5. For use in the following tasks, make two copies of this document. Use **File-Save As** and save one copy as *Report1*; repeat and save the second copy as *Report2*. Close all documents.

Controlling page breaks using paragraph formatting

Page breaks can also be controlled through the pagination section of the **Format-Paragraph-Line and Page Breaks** dialog box.

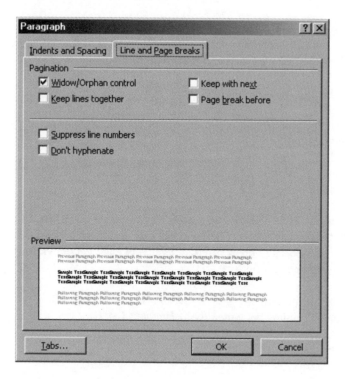

There are four types of formatting available:

❏   Word exercises widow and orphan control if the **Widow/Orphan control** box is checked; that is to say, it will prevent widows and orphans from occurring. A widow is a single line at the beginning of a paragraph left at the bottom of a page and an orphan is a single line at the end of a paragraph at the top of a page.

❏   **Keep lines together**: Use this to prevent a page break anywhere within a paragraph.

❏   **Keep with next**: Use this to prevent a page break occurring between a paragraph and the following one: for example, to keep a sub-heading with its following paragraph or to keep the lines of a table together.

❏   **Page break before**: If a paragraph such as a heading is formatted with this, then a page break will be inserted before the paragraph. If each chapter of your document is to appear on a new page then format the chapter heading with **Page break before** by clicking in the appropriate check box. To remove this page break the formatting must be removed from the paragraph.

By making use of these formatting options the need for hard pages breaks to be inserted in a long document can be eliminated. When the document is altered the page breaks will follow the rules applied in the paragraph formatting and consequently should occur in sensible places.

Task 3: Using soft breaks

The hard breaks originally put into the document *Report* are to be replaced by soft breaks controlled by the type of paragraph formatting.

1.   Open the document *Report* in Normal view.

2.   Remove the hard page break at the end of the title page by selecting it and pressing the *Delete* key.

3.   Position the insertion point in the heading 'Terms of Reference'. Change the paragraph style to *Heading 1*.

4.   Use **Format-Style** and click on **Modify, Format** and **Paragraph**. Click on the **Page break before** check box. Click on **OK** twice and then on **Apply**. In Normal view you should see a soft break inserted. Switch to Page Layout view or use **File-Print Preview** to verify the effect.

5.   Replace all the remaining hard breaks with soft breaks. Remove each one and change the heading paragraph to the *Heading 1* style.

6.   Save the document *Report*.

Page numbering

There are two methods of inserting page numbers:

❏ Page numbers may be inserted using **Insert-Page Numbers**. Page numbers may be placed at the bottom of the page (footer) or at the top of the page (header). The alignment of the number can be chosen and whether or not all pages are to be numbered except the first. Remove the tick from the **Show number on first page** check box to omit the number from the first page. This is useful for documents that have a title page as the first page.

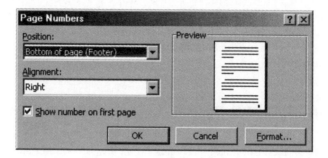

❏ Page numbers may be inserted as part of a header or footer (discussed later in this unit).

Task 4: Page numbering

In this task you will apply page numbering to the document *Report1*.

1. Use **Insert-Page Numbers** to add page numbers to the document.

2. Check that **Position: Bottom of page** (footer) and **Alignment: Center** are selected.

3. Click on the **Format** button and choose numbering to **Start at 0**. This is so that the second page will have a page number of 1. Click on **OK**.

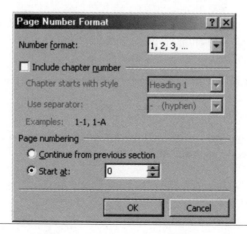

4. Click on **Show number on first page** to remove the tick; this prevents the first page number from displaying. Click on **OK**.

5. Choose **View-Page Layout**. In Page Layout view the page numbers should be visible at the bottom of each page.

6. Use **File-Print Preview** to see the effect.

7. Save the document *Report1*.

    If the page numbers are not visible when the document is previewed, then their position in the bottom margin may need adjusting. To do this choose **File-Page Setup** and increase the distance of the header or footer from the edge (see below). You may also need to adjust the position of the top and bottom margins to accommodate the change.

Printing specified pages

You do not have to print the whole document; you can print just a selection of pages. In the Print dialog box click on the **Pages** option button. In the associated text box list the page numbers to be printed. For example, to print pages 5, 7 and 9 simply type *5,7,9*; to print pages 5 to 8 inclusive type *5-8*.

Headers and footers

A *header* is text or graphics that appears at the top of every page. A *footer* appears at the bottom of every page. Headers and footers are useful in long documents as they can be used to indicate, for example, the chapter or section title. In business documents they may contain a reference number or company logo. If the work is an assignment, a header or footer could be used to put the author's name on each page. Word prints headers in the top margin and footers in the bottom margin.

As well as being able to add headers and footers that are the same on every page, Word also offers choices of customising headers and footers.

❑ If the document is to be printed on both sides of the paper then headers and footers can be set up so that even numbered pages have one header and odd numbered pages have a different one.

❑ If the first page of the document is different from the rest of the document, for example a title page, then headers and footers can be set so that they are different on the first page.

 ❑ If the document is divided into sections then different headers and footers can be applied to each section. Sections are discussed in Unit 11.

 You can change the appearance of headers and footers (font, typeface etc.) by modifying the *Header* and *Footer* styles for the document.

Adding or removing a header or footer

To add a header or footer to your document, use **View-Header and Footer**. The document switches to a page layout view with the text of each page shown in grey (or lighter than normal) and a Header and Footer toolbar appears.

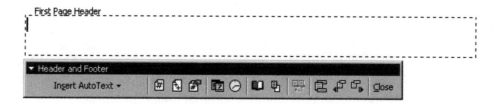

Headers and footers have preset tabs. There is a centre tab in the middle of the page and a right tab at the right edge of the page. By using the preset tabs, the headers or footers will be consistent through the document. Select a suitable font for your header or footer, tab across to the position required and type in the text. Using the buttons, as described below, enter text for headers and footers as required. When finished, click on **Close**.

Icons and buttons in the Header and Footer toolbar

The first button on the Header and Footer toolbar allows you to insert AutoText. The next three buttons are:

❏ Insert page numbering

❏ Insert number of pages

❏ Format page number

The next two buttons are:

❏ Insert date

❏ Insert time

To put the date, time, page number or number of pages into a header or footer, position the insertion point and then click on the appropriate icon.

The next two buttons are **Page Setup** and **Show/Hide Document Text**. Clicking on **Page Setup** will display the **Page Setup** dialog box. Clicking on **Show/Hide Document Text** will toggle between showing or hiding the document text.

The next button is the **Same as Previous** button. Click on this button if the header or footer is to be different from the header or footer in the previous section. Unit 11 discusses dividing the document up into sections.

The first button of the final group of three allows you to switch between the header and footer. The next two buttons allow forward and backward movement between different headers or footers. There will only be different headers and footers if **Different first page** or **Different odd and even** have been selected in **Page Setup** or if there are different sections in the document.

When the text for the header or footer has been typed in, click on the **Close** button to return to the document text body.

Before printing it is a good idea to preview the document. Headers and footers can be positioned by choosing **File-Page Setup** and defining their required position in the **From edge** section of the **Margins** tab on the Page Setup dialog box.

Page numbering in headers or footers

Page numbering can be controlled by clicking on the **Page Number Format** button in the Header and Footer toolbar or through using **Insert-Page Numbers** and clicking on the **Format** button. The Page Number Format dialog box will be displayed.

The format of page numbering may be chosen from the **Number Format** box, i.e. Arabic or Roman numerals or alphabetic numbering. It is also possible to alter the number at which page numbering starts. This can be useful if the document is long and is stored as separate files. The start page number of the second and subsequent files may be altered accordingly. Different formats of page numbering may be used in different sections of a document.

Editing or removing existing headers and footers

To remove or edit an existing header or footer:

1. Use **View-Header and Footer** and display either the header or footer using the ⬚ (**Switch Between Header and Footer**) button.

2. Edit the text in the header or footer in the normal fashion. Text may be pasted into the header or footer, or copied from it. To remove the header or footer, simply delete all the text.

3. Click on **Close**.

Task 5: Headers and footers

In this task a header and footer are added to the document *Questionnaires*. Open the document.

1. Choose **View-Header and Footer** and the insertion point is ready positioned in the header.

2. Press the _Tab_ key to move to the centre tab and type in the text 'Adjusting Margins'.

3. Click on the ▣ (**Switch Between Header and Footer**) button to display the footer.

4. Press the _Tab_ key twice to move to the right tab and type in your name.

5. Click on **Close**.

6. Preview the document and make any adjustments to the positions of the header and footer as described above. Also view the document in Page Layout view to see the header and footer. Save the document as **Questionnaires** and print it.

7. From Normal view use **View-Header and Footer** and display the footer.

8. Select the footer text and delete it.

9. Click on **Close**. Preview the document or use Page Layout view to see the effect. It is not necessary to save this change.

Different header and footer on the first page

You can have a header and footer on the first page that are different to those of later pages. To select this option:

1. Choose **View-Header and Footer** and click on the ▣ (**Page Setup**) button.

2. Click in the **Different first page** check box. This will create a First Header and a First Footer as well as the normal Header and Footer. The text in a First Header may be different from the Header and the text in a First Footer may be different from the Footer.

3. Use the ▣ button and the ▣ (**Show Next**) and ▣ (**Show Previous**) buttons to navigate to the required header or footer and key in the text.

4. Click on **Close**.

Task 6: Making headers and footers different on the first page

Using the document _Report2_, this task adds a header and a footer both of which will not appear on the first page of the document. Page numbering is incorporated into the footer.

1. Use the Page Number Format dialog box available through **Insert-Page Numbers** to start the page numbering at 0 so that the first page of text will appear to be page 1. Click on **OK** and **Close**.

2. Choose **View-Header and Footer**.

3. Click on the 🖳 (**Page Setup**) button. Click on the **Different first page** check box and click on **OK**.

4. Use the 🖳 (**Show Next**) button to move to Header from First Header.

5. Press the *Tab* key once and key in the text 'Fitness Suite Feasibility Study'.

6. Move to the Footer (not the First Footer).

7. Press the *Tab* key once and click on the page numbering icon.

8. Press *Tab* again and key in your name.

9. Click on **Close**.

10. Save the document as *Report2*.

At this point review and compare the documents *Report1* and *Report2*. If you wish, make extra copies of the document *Report* and experiment with headers and footers.

Odd and even headers and footers

Odd and even headers and footers are used when the finished document will be produced like a book, where both sides of the paper are printed. In a book, left-hand pages are even numbered and right-hand pages are odd numbered. A header or footer can be defined so that it reads across from an even to an odd page. Different information about the document can appear on odd and even pages: for example, chapter title on even pages and section title on odd pages. To achieve this:

1. Choose **View-Header and Footer** and click on the 🖳 (**Page Setup**) button.

2. Click on the **Different odd and even** check box. This will create an Even Header, an Odd Header, an Even Footer and an Odd Footer. The text in the Even Header may be different from the Odd Header and the text in the Even Footer may be different from the Odd Footer.

3. Use the 🖳 button and the 🖳 (**Show Next**) and 🖳 (**Show Previous**) buttons to navigate to the required header or footer and key in the text.

4. Click on **Close**.

Note that the **Different odd and even** option may be used in conjunction with the **Different first page** option.

Footnotes and endnotes

Footnotes and endnotes are notes of reference, explanation or comment. A word in the main text can be marked with a footnote or endnote reference mark. A number is commonly used for a reference mark. Footnotes are found at the bottom of the page and endnotes are found at the end of the document. Word allows footnotes and endnotes of any length to be added to a document.

Text used in a footnote can be formatted just as any other text. To add a footnote or endnote:

1. In Normal view, first position the insertion point at the end of the word that the footnote or endnote is to refer to.

2. Use **Insert-Footnote**. The Footnote and Endnote dialog box appears.

3. Click on either **Footnote** or **Endnote** to select the type of note. Click on **OK** and a footnote pane appears as shown below. A reference mark is positioned in the document at the position of the insertion point.

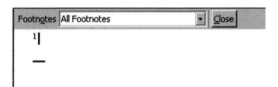

4. Key in the text. The insertion point is ready positioned following the reference mark.

5. Click on **Close**.

As footnotes or endnotes are added Word automatically numbers them. Word will automatically renumber footnote/endnote and reference marks whenever footnotes/endnotes are added, deleted or moved.

Alternatively, you can choose your own labelling system by clicking on the **Custom mark** option in the Footnote and Endnote dialog box. The **Symbols** button allows you to choose the character to be used as a marker.

Splitting a Document into Sections

What you will learn in this unit

This unit contains further activities associated with long documents. At the end of this unit you will be able to:

❑ Divide a document into sections.

❑ Generate a contents list.

By dividing a document up into sections, different formatting such as different headers and footers, page numbering and orientation or layout can be achieved. A document can be divided into any number of sections and a section can be of any length. A section can be as short as one paragraph or as long as the whole document.

If the standard heading styles are used in the document, Word can use these to create a table of contents for the document.

What you need

To complete this unit you will need:

❑ The document file *Report* created in Unit 10

Dividing the document into sections

You may divide a document into sections after you have keyed in all the text or you can create sections as you work. If this is new to you then it is advisable to perform this activity when the text of the document is complete. To put a section break into a document use **Insert-Break**.

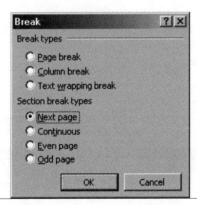

From the dialog box select a section break from the choices available.

❏ A section break may be chosen so that it starts on the next page, or so that there is no apparent break. This is the **Continuous** option.

❏ To start a new section on the next page select the **Next page** option.

❏ If the document is to be printed on both sides of the page then you may want to start a new section on either the next odd or even page. This choice can be made by clicking on the appropriate option button.

Word separates each section with a section break, which appears in Normal view as a double dotted line across the screen with text describing the type of break, for example 'End of Section (Next Page)', in its centre. A new section should be created when a change occurs in the document. For example:

❏ The number of newspaper-style columns on a page changes. Here a Continuous section break should be used.

❏ The alignment of the text changes between portrait and landscape. Here a Next Page section break should be used.

❏ The format, sequence and position of page numbering changes. Use any break except Continuous.

❏ The text and formatting of headers and footers changes. Use any break except Continuous.

Applying different formatting to individual sections

Once the document has been divided up into sections then different formatting may be applied.

Headers and footers

Using **View-Header and Footer** and the 📖 (**Page Setup**) button you can specify the types of headers and footers required in each section of your document. If the header or footer is the same as that in the previous section then click on the 🔳 (**Same as Previous**) button.

Two headers are illustrated below. The header area is enclosed by a dashed bounding rectangle with information about the type of header, the section number and whether it is the same as the previous header.

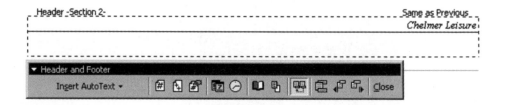

Footers are shown in a similar way.

Task 1: Creating sections and applying different headers and footers

This task shows how different headers and footers may be applied to different sections of a document. Open the document *Report*, created in Unit 10.

1. Position the insertion point at the left of the heading 'Findings from market research'.

2. Choose **Insert-Break**.

3. Click on **Next page**. A double dotted line with the text 'Section Break (Next Page)' appears on the screen above the heading.

The disadvantages of questionnaires are that there may be a low response, questions usually have to be simple and straightforward and if they are anonymous then there is no information about the person who has answered them.

==Section Break (Next Page)=========

FINDINGS FROM MARKET RESEARCH

Information has been collated from the returned questionnaires resulting in:

- a consensus of opinion that present facilities are inadequate and that attendance is poor

---

4. Use **View-Header and Footer**, click on the ▥ (**Page Setup**) button and check that **Different first page** does not have a tick in its box. Click on **Close**.

5. In the Header Section 2 area click on the ▤ (**Same as Previous**) button so that the header is different to the previous one. Overwrite any existing heading with the text 'Findings' on the right-hand side. Click on **Close**.

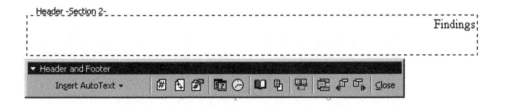

6. Modify the *Header* paragraph style, so that it is Times New Roman, 10-point italic.

7. Save the document as *Report*. Use **File-Print Preview** in **two pages** mode to view the document. Print out the last three pages.

Page numbering

Each section may have its own page numbering. To customise a section make sure the insertion point is in the section to be customised. Use **Insert-Page Numbers** and alter the page numbering in the Page Numbers dialog box.

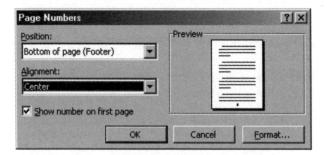

Click on the **Format** button to change the start number.

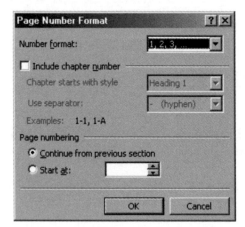

Page layout

Different sections may have different formatting; for example the orientation, page size or number of columns can alter. Note that paragraph styles remain the same regardless of section breaks. If you want to use different fonts in a particular section then define additional style names.

Task 2: Creating sections using different orientations

1. Start a new document. Select **File-Page Setup**, click on the **Paper Size** tab and select the **Landscape** option. Click on **OK**. Key in the following text and save it as *Timetable*. Close the document.

	Chelmer Leisure and Recreation Centre				
	ACTIVITY PROGRAMME				
FITNESS SUITE	**Monday**	**Tuesday**	**Wednesday**	**Thursday**	**Friday**
Daytime					
10-11.00am	Ladies Aerobics	Mens Multi-gym	Ladies Aerobics		Body Conditioning
11.00-12.00pm	Weight Training			Weight Training	Step Aerobics
2.00-3.00pm		Ladies Multi-gym	Body Conditioning	Step Aerobics	Mens Multi-gym
3.00-4.00pm	Body Conditioning		Weight Training	Multi-gym	
Evening					
7.00-9.00pm	Step Aerobics	Family Multi-gym	Weight Training	Body Conditioning	

2. Start a second document. This two-page document will have the first page in portrait orientation and the second in landscape. Key in the following text. Save the file as *Timetable Memo*.

CHELMER LEISURE AND RECREATION CENTRE

MEMORANDUM

To: All Multi-gym Staff   Date: 8 October 2001

From: Geoff Richards

MULTI-GYM ACTIVITY PROGRAMME

Further to last Wednesday's meeting I have completed the activity timetable for the multi-gym. A copy is attached to this memo. Thank you for your hard work and co-operation in devising activity programmes to be used in the multi-gym.

---

3. Press *Enter* to make a new line and use **Insert-Break** to insert a section break starting on the next page.

4. Select **File-Page Setup** and click on **Landscape** orientation in the **Paper Size** tab. The **Apply to** box should show 'This section' (see below).

5. Using **Insert-File** insert the document *Timetable* created in step 1. Adjust the table to fill the page. Note that you will need to scroll left and right to view the width of the page, or use the zoom facility to 'shrink' the view.

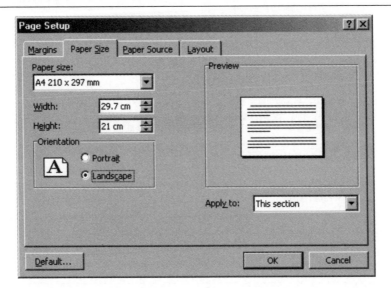

6. View the document using **File-Print Preview** in **two pages** mode. The first page should be displayed in portrait orientation and the second in landscape. Print out the document; do not save it.

Creating a simple table of contents

Most large documents have headings. Some headings are more important than others; for example a chapter heading is more important than a paragraph heading. Word allows nine heading styles to be defined. *Heading 1* is the most important and *Heading 9* is the least important. Usually two or three heading styles are enough for a document.

By defining and using the heading styles for your documents, not only is consistency maintained but Word is also able to use them to create a table of contents. This is best illustrated in the following task.

Task 3: Creating a table of contents

A simple table of contents is to be created for the document *Report*.

1. Open the document *Report*.

2. Choose and define a style for *Heading 1*.

3. Apply this style to the heading at the top of each page (if you have not already done so).

4. Save the document.

5. Position the insertion point where the table of contents is to go. Tables of contents may be put anywhere.

6. Use *Ctrl/End* to move to the end of the document. Type **Contents** on a new line and format this with page break before. Change the style to *Heading 2*.

7. Position the cursor under 'Contents', choose **Insert-Index and Tables** and click on the **Table of Contents** tab.

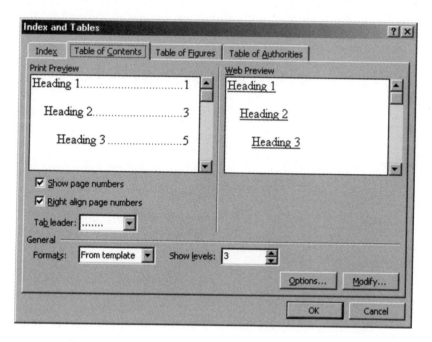

8. Change the **Show levels** value to 1, so that only *Heading 1* is used in the contents. Click on **OK**. The table of contents will be inserted.

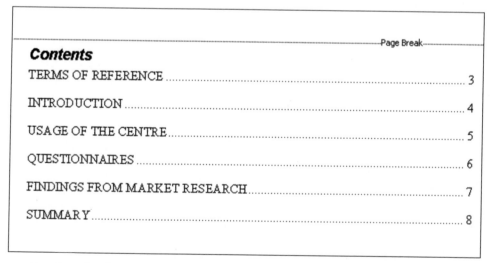

9. Save the document as *Report*. Should the document be revised, the table of contents can be updated by positioning the insertion point at the start of the table of

contents and pressing _F9_. You will be given the choice of updating either just the page numbers or the whole table of contents.

 Note: You can use a table of contents to 'jump' to a specific heading in your document by clicking on the heading or its page number in the contents list.

Working with Windows and Templates

What you will learn in this unit

When using a word processor such as Word it is likely that on some occasions you will be creating more than one document at a time. This module explains how to manage and work with more than one open document. At the end of this unit you will be able to:

❑ Use multiple windows.

❑ Move text between documents.

❑ Interface with other software.

❑ Set up and use a document template.

Working in a Windows environment makes it possible for different portions of a document to be viewed on the screen at the same time. It also makes it possible to work with more than one document at once.

What you need

To complete this unit you will need:

❑ The document file *Terms of Reference* created in Unit 3 and amended in Unit 4.

❑ The document file *Centre Introduction* created in Unit 3.

❑ The document file *Centre Usage* created in Unit 3.

Splitting the document window

By splitting the document window different parts of the same document can be seen on the screen at the same time. This is useful if the portion being written refers to an earlier portion. Viewing the earlier portion while writing the current portion can save scrolling up and down through the document. An earlier part of the document may be copied to a later part and this task is simplified by viewing both parts of the document on screen at the same time.

To split the document:

1. Move the mouse pointer to the small bar at the top of the vertical scrollbar. The pointer changes shape to two horizontal lines with arrows.

2. While the pointer is this shape click and drag a horizontal line downwards. Position the line approximately halfway down the document window and release.

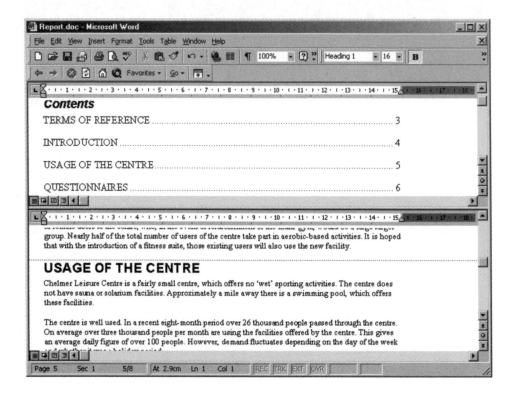

At the right-hand edge of the window the vertical scrollbar now appears as two separate scrollbars, one for each portion of the split. It is possible to scroll each split portion independently, thereby positioning an earlier portion of the document on the screen at the same time as a later one. Note that each portion has its own ruler.

To remove a split:

1. Move the mouse pointer to the bar between the two vertical scrollbars. The pointer changes shape to two horizontal lines with arrows.

2. While the pointer is this shape click and drag the split line upwards to the top of the document screen area, then release.

More than one window onto the same document

Another way of viewing two parts of a document at the same time is to use more than one window. This can provide more flexibility and be useful when working with larger documents. If, for example, you wished to refer to more than one page of the document then it would be useful to be able to switch between several views of the different pages.

To set up another window onto the document use **Window-New Window**. Word redisplays the document and the title of the document is altered by the addition of :2. This is the window number. Every time **Window-New Window** is used a new window onto the document is created.

To see a list of the windows that have been created open the **Window** menu. The list of open windows is in the lower section of this menu. To switch to another window simply click on the name of the appropriate one in the Window list or click on the corresponding button in the Windows taskbar.

File-Close closes the document and all associated windows. To close a document's specific windows use the ⊠ button for those windows. The shortcut key to close a document window is *Ctrl/w*.

To view several windows on the screen at the same time use **Window-Arrange All**. The windows can be positioned by moving and sizing them. However, the screen can become rather cluttered. For this reason it is advisable to have no more than four windows open. Only one window can be active at once. If the default Windows colours are being used then the active window has a blue title bar. To change the active window simply click on the one to be made active.

A document window may be in one of three 'Windows' states, i.e. it may be maximised (fills application window), restored (smaller than the application window) or minimised (appearing only on the taskbar). You can control the Windows state of your document window by clicking on the ⊡, ⧉ and ⧄ buttons.

Cutting and copying between windows

Copy or cut and paste operations can be carried out between windows. First switch to the window containing the portion of the document that is to be cut or copied. Select the section and use **Edit-Cut** (*Ctrl/x*) or **Edit-Copy** (*Ctrl/c*) to transfer the text to the clipboard.

Next switch to the window into which the contents of the clipboard are to be pasted by using the **Window** menu, or make it active by clicking in it. Position the insertion point and choose **Edit-Paste** (or *Ctrl/v*).

Working with more than one document

All that has been described about using more than one window onto a document can be applied to using more than one document. Instead of using **Window-New Window** to open more windows onto the document, use **File-Open** to open all the documents required. To see a list of all open documents open the **Window** menu; use **Window-Arrange All** if you wish to see all document windows arranged on the screen at the same time.

Copy or cut and paste operations can be carried out as described previously. Note that portions that are pasted into a document retain the font and formatting that was applied in the original document.

Task 1: Working with windows

To perform this task close any documents that you may have open using **File-Close**. When all documents are closed the application workspace is empty.

1. Open the file *Terms of Reference*.

2. Open the file *Centre Introduction*.

3. Choose **Window-Arrange All**. Both documents should be visible on the screen, each occupying its own window and taking up half the screen display.

4. Open the file *Centre Usage*. Open the **Window** menu and notice that all of the open documents are listed. Select **Arrange All** (see opposite).

5. The screen has become cluttered so close *Terms of Reference* (click anywhere in the *Terms of Reference* document window to make it active) by clicking on the ☒ button for that window.

6. Use **Window-Arrange All** to reposition the remaining document windows.

7. Next, copy text from one window to another. Make *Centre Introduction* active by clicking in its window. Press *Ctrl/End* to move the insertion point to the end of the document.

8. Make *Centre Usage* active. Highlight the first paragraph and use **Edit-Copy**.

9. Make *Centre Introduction* active, check that the insertion point is at the end of the document and use **Edit-Paste**.

10. Close the documents but do not save the changes.

11. Open two of the documents again and experiment with minimising, maximising and restoring them. If you can't find a document because it is hidden behind another document window then open the **Window** menu to locate it.

12. Close these two documents.

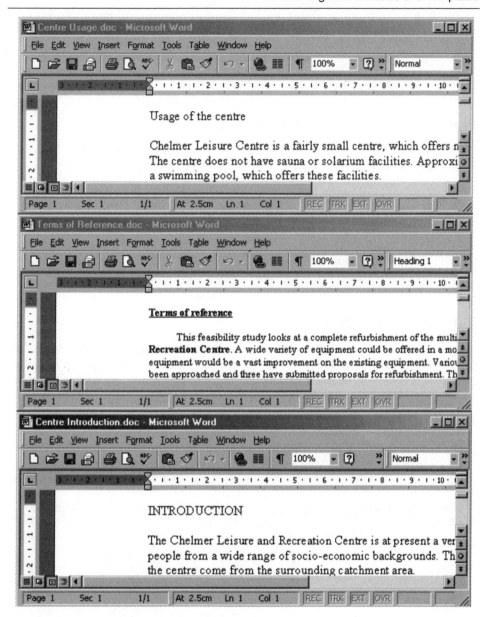

Interfacing with other software

Word interfaces well with other Windows applications, particularly those written by Microsoft. It will also interface with other software.

Importing text files

It is possible to import text that has been directly created by another word processor or by previous versions of Word. When **File-Open** is used, select *All Files (*.*)* from the **Files of type** list box to list all files in the directory. Many word processors produce documents files with the extension *.doc* but text files may have other extensions such as *.txt* or *.rtf.*

If a file is selected that was not created by Word, then Word will automatically convert it.

Exporting files for use with other software

To export files, use **File-Save As** and open the **Save as type** list box. Select the type of format required and save in the usual way. For example, the document can be saved in WordPerfect format.

Interfacing with other Windows applications

Within windows the clipboard can be used to import text or graphics from other Windows applications. For example, you can import tables from Excel or graphics from the Windows Paint application via the clipboard.

Creating templates

A *template* is a predefined format for a document. Many business documents such as letters, memos, forms and reports have set formats. A template can be used to define not only standard text but also aspects such as the font, borders, page size and orientation. Once a template has been created it can be recalled and used to produce the required document. This saves time and ensures consistency.

Word comes with many predefined templates and several wizards to help you create documents such as letters and memos. To create most documents the 'normal document' template *Normal.dot* is used. This is the template that you have been

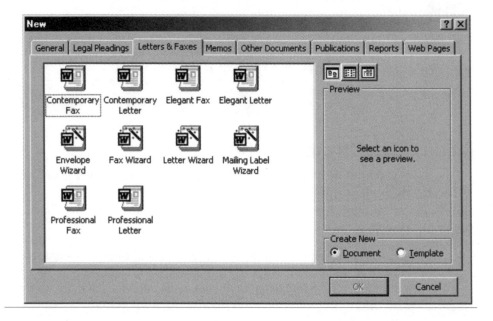

using to create your documents. If a document is started using **File-New** then a dialog box containing the names of the templates appears. These are grouped by type, which you select by clicking on the appropriate tab. Under the **General** tab you can select the normal template file by choosing *Blank Document*. Template files have the extension *.dot* and are stored in the Word template folder.

Word provides other template files, such as a standard letter and memo, and it is possible to customise these. However, Task 2 will concentrate on producing a custom template based on the normal template. The template will contain standard text. Standard text is often referred to as *boilerplate* text.

Task 2: Creating a template

There are several ways of creating a template; the one that will be used for this task will create a template from the document that is being worked on. The template will be set up based upon Word's normal template, which is the one usually used for document creation.

1. Start a new document and key in the following text, leaving the prices blank.

Chelmer Leisure and Recreation Centre
Multi-Gym

Price per session

Adult

Junior

Concessionary

Club Adult

Club Junior

---

2. Save this as a template rather than a document. Use **File-Save**, and in the Save As dialog box open the **Save as type** box and choose **Document Template**. Type *Multi-Gym Prices* in the **File name** box and click on **Save**. Close the template document.

3. To use this template for the creation of a new document (e.g. when the prices change), start a new document using **File-New**.

4. Select from the **General** tab in the dialog box and click on the icon labelled *Multi-Gym Prices*.

5. The boilerplate text and formatting will appear and the prices can be filled in and the document saved and printed in the usual manner.

Template files can be recalled and edited by using **File-Open** and selecting **Document Templates** in the **Files of type** list box. Template files are normally stored in a separate *Templates* folder, not in your working folder. If you use a networked version of Word then custom templates may be stored in an alternative folder. Check with your network manager.

Task 3: Storing styles in templates

The flexibility of templates can be further increased by defining a set of styles that can be stored with a template. In fact it is possible to have a template without any text. The default template *Normal* is an example. It contains Word's standard styles.

The styles defined for the title page could also be used for title pages of other pieces of work. These styles can be saved as a template which can be applied to future documents. This task uses a straightforward method for setting up a style template.

1. Open a new document using **File-New** and click on **More Word Templates** to display the template icons.

2. Select the **Template** option button.

3. Choose *Blank Document* from the list of templates as the new template is to be based on this template. Click on **OK**.

4. Type the word ***Title1*** with your preferred formatting and set up the style *Title1* as described in Unit 6 Task 2.

5. Repeat for each style (e.g. on the next line type ***Title2*** and set up the style *Title2*).

6. Use **File-Save As** and type ***Titles*** in the **File name** box. This file is saved as a *.dot* template file. Close the file using **File-Close**.

7. To use this template, start a new document using **File-New-More Word Templates** and select *Titles* from the list of templates (see opposite). Replace the words 'Title1', 'Title2' etc. with the required titles. It is not necessary to use all of the styles each time a front page is created. Save the new title page in the usual manner.

You can combine text and style in a template, for example, the name of the institution could be used instead of 'Title1'. You could remove the text in the template before saving, i.e. before the last step above, to leave just the style definitions in the template.

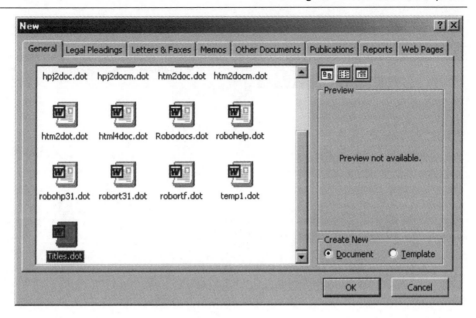

Adding styles to a template

As a document is created styles may be defined which would be useful to be stored. These may be added to the document template by clicking in the **Add to template** check box in the bottom left-hand corner of the New Style or Modify Style dialog box. When you save your document Word will ask if you wish to save the changes to the template.

If you wish new styles to be added to the template file, or copied from one document to another, then this can be done using the Organizer dialog box, which is available from the **Format-Style** command. In the list on the left of the dialog box the styles used in the active document or its template are shown. Styles used in the *Normal* document template are listed on the right.

If you wish to use styles that have been stored in a template or document which is different from the template currently being used, then the styles from that template can be copied into the current document. This can also be achieved using the Organizer dialog box.

Task 4: Copying styles

In this task the styles created and saved in the template *Titles.dot* are to be merged into the document *Report*.

1. Open the document file *Report*.

2. Use **Format-Style** and click on **Organizer**.

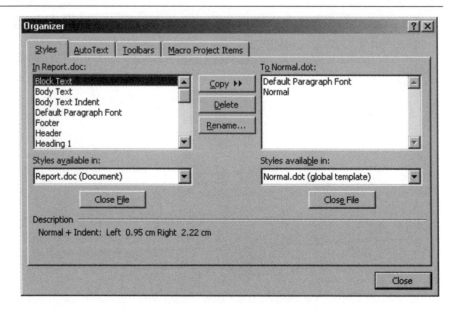

3. Click on **Close File** on the right side of the dialog box. Next click on **Open File** and select the template *Titles.dot*.

   Note: You may select either a document or a template from which to copy styles. The Open dialog box allows you to change drive or directory, or to list document or template files.

4 Select *Title1* from the list of style names and click on **<< Copy**. Repeat for other styles in this document that you may wish to copy.

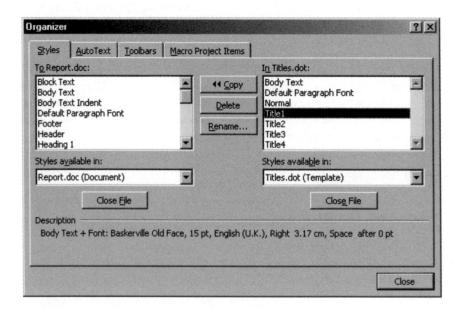

5   Click on **Close**.

6. Open the style list box (on the formatting toolbar) and the styles you copied are listed.

7. Apply these to the title page. Select each portion of the title page in turn, open the style list box and choose the appropriate style.

8. Save the document *Report*.

Checking Spelling and Grammar

What you will learn in this unit

This unit shows how you can check your document for errors and reduce mistake while you type. At the end of this unit you will be able to:

❑   Check spelling.

❑   Make automatic corrections as you type.

❑   Use the thesaurus.

❑   Use the grammar checker.

❑   Make AutoText entries.

There are various ways in which the word processor can help to improve the text in a document. Many word processor users are not trained typists and are prone to make errors while keying in their work. Word will check your work as you key it in. Mistakes are shown with a wiggly line underneath so that you can instantly revise them by clicking on the word with the right mouse button, which generates a shortcut menu. The spell-check facility will provide suggestions for the correct spelling if you are not sure. Even so, it is good practice to check your document for spelling and grammatical mistakes before printing the final copy. The word processor can only apply limited rules to a document so after checking the spelling and grammar always proofread your work. If the work would benefit from rewording use the thesaurus to help.

Checking spelling and grammar as you work

You will already have noticed Word's ability to check your spelling and grammar as you type. Spelling errors are underlined with a red wavy line and grammatical errors with a green wavy line. Transposing letters while typing often causes a spelling mistake, and a typing error such as this can easily be amended. However, there will be a number of occasions when Word will not recognise a word because it is not in its dictionary.

Where a spelling error is marked, point to the word and click the *right* mouse button. This displays a shortcut menu, which will suggest alternatives, allow you to ignore all occurrences of the word, add the word to the dictionary or start the spell checker.

Where a grammatical error is marked, point to any of the underlined words and click the *right* mouse button. This displays a shortcut menu that will suggest alternatives, allow you to ignore the error or start the grammar checker.

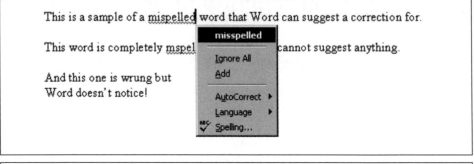

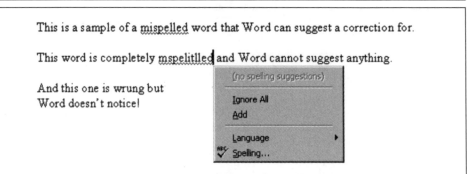

Task 1: Correcting spelling as you work

In a new document experiment by keying in deliberately misspelt words and point to these words. Click on the right mouse button to see the shortcut menu. Just use the suggestions and **Ignore All**; do not add any words to the dictionary or start the spell checker. Close the document without saving it.

Using the spelling and grammar checker

The spell checker can be used to check a selection or the whole document. If a selection is to be checked, select it first. The spell checker is activated in any of the following ways:

❑ Select **Tools-Spelling and Grammar**.

❑ Click on the **Spelling and Grammar** button.

❑ Use the shortcut key *F7*.

❑ Choose **Spelling** from the right-click shortcut menu.

If you have not made a selection Word will start the spell check from the position of the insertion point. The Spelling and Grammar dialog box appears.

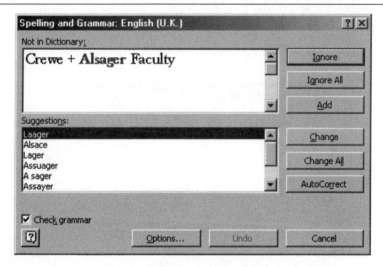

Both spelling and grammar are checked, but if you only wish to check the spelling then remove the tick from the **Check grammar** box.

When the spell checker comes across a word it does not recognise it shows it in the **Not in Dictionary** box. In the **Suggestions** box the spell checker offers a correction, or a list of possible corrections. Behind the spelling dialog box the document can be seen with the word in question highlighted.

There are a number of options available, shown by the buttons.

❏ If the correct spelling is in the **Suggestions** box click to highlight it and click on the **Change** button.

❏ If you think that the mistake may be repeated throughout the document then use the **Change All** button instead of the **Change** button.

❏ If the word is correct but is not in the spell checker's dictionary then choose **Ignore** or you may **Add** the word to the dictionary. Consult the Office Assistant for information about adding to or creating your own dictionary. Use **Ignore All** to ignore all occurrences of the word throughout the document.

❏ If you want Word to automatically correct the mistake if you make it again while typing then click on the **AutoCorrect** button. AutoCorrect is discussed in more detail later in this unit.

❏ You can customise the spelling and grammatical rules used for checking by clicking on the **Options** button.

Unless a block of text is selected, the spell checker will check the entire document, and when finished will return to the original place of the insertion point. If you are checking a selection, when that is finished you have the option to carry on and check the whole document.

Grammar will be checked if the **Check grammar** box is ticked. If the grammar checker finds a sentence with questionable grammar or style, it displays it in the dialog box as shown below.

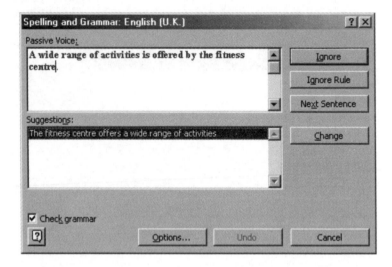

Words related to the suspected error are displayed in coloured (default green) type. The grammar checker displays suggested corrections in the **Suggestions** box. Choices of action are:

❑ Make a suggested correction. Select one of the corrections from the **Suggestions** box and click on the **Change** button.

❑ Make your own corrections in the document. Make the document window active by clicking on it. Edit the sentence and click on the **Resume** button in the dialog box to resume checking the document.

❑ Ignore the questioned word or sentence without making changes. Click on the **Ignore** button.

❑ Ignore all occurrences of this error in the document. Click on the **Ignore All** button.

❑ Skip the entire sentence. Click on the **Next Sentence** button to start checking the next sentence.

Task 2: Correcting grammar as you work

The following piece of text is deliberately incorrect. Key it into a new document exactly. As each mistake is highlighted, point and click with the right mouse button and correct the text. You should find 'Atlanta's' suggested for 'Atlantas' and 'it's' for 'its'. However, the grammar checker does not pick up the fact that 'There' should be 'Their'.

Atlantas proposal was the one considered the most attractive for Chelmer Leisure and Recreation Centre. The Athena equipment offers a great advantage due to the nature of it's design. There equipment is designed so that it can be positioned 'back to back' to save valuable space.

Task 3: Checking a document for spelling and grammatical errors

The following piece of text is also deliberately incorrect. Key it into the document you used for the last task. Note that the word 'colour' is deliberately spelt the American way and will be highlighted if the English (U.K.) dictionary is being used. To check which dictionary is in use, choose **Tools-Language-Set Language**. If English (U.K.) is not being used then select the whole document and set English (U.K.) using **Tools-Language-Set Language**. If this is a problem check your Regional Settings in the Windows Control Panel.

Correct the piece as you see fit. You may either accept changes or try rewording the piece. It is not necessary to save this.

Plastic credit cards would be issued to the members, one color indicating full and another to indicate concessionary members. These would be signed by the user and handed in at the reception by the member while they use the facility. Each card would be printed with the details of the membership and times for the use by the member. Each occasion a member uses the facility it would be recorded by the receptionist, to monitor usage of the scheme.

AutoCorrect

You can tell Word about your common typing mistakes so that, as you type, Word will monitor your typing for these mistakes and automatically correct them. Word maintains a list of common 'mistypes' and their corrections and Word will correct you, if you mistype a word from this list. For example the word 'occurrance' would be corrected as 'occurrence'. If you do not wish Word to do this then you can switch off this feature using **Tools-AutoCorrect** and remove the cross from the **Replace text as you type** check box.

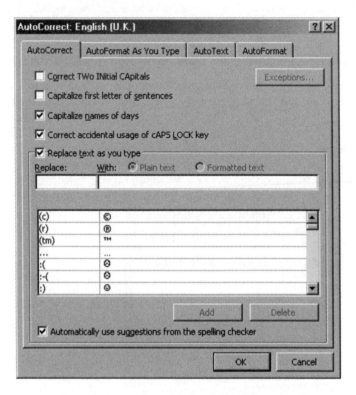

You may add 'mistype' words and their corrections to the AutoCorrect list, either through using **Tools-AutoCorrect** or by clicking on the **AutoCorrect** button in the Spelling dialog box.

The AutoCorrect dialog box also offers the following corrections, which you may switch on or off by either ticking the appropriate check box or leaving it blank:

❏ Correction of two capitals at the beginning of a word (may happen if you type quickly and do not release the *Shift* key soon enough).

❏ Capitalisation of the first word of a sentence.

❏ Capitalisation of the names of the days of the week.

❏ Correction of typing when *Caps Lock* has been left on and the first word is lower case and the rest upper case (it also switches off *Caps Lock*).

Task 4: Correcting spelling

For this task, open the document *Centre Introduction*.

1. Click on the ✓ button and check your spelling.

2. If you correct any errors save the document before closing it.

3. Try this with other files you have created, e.g. *Centre Usage*, *Terms of Reference* and *Questionnaires*.

Task 5: Making an AutoCorrect entry

1. Choose **Tools-AutoCorrect** and select the **AutoCorrect** tab. See that the **Replace text as you type** check box is checked. You will see that Word already has quite a comprehensive list of spelling and keying mistakes and their corrections.

2. In the **Replace** box type 'usualy' (this is an example of a common mistake).

3. In the **With** box type 'usually' (the correct spelling) and click on **Add**. Click on **OK**.

4. In a new document that you do not save experiment with misspelling this word. You may add other words that you commonly mistype, which are not already in the AutoCorrect list. Try adding 'item' to replace 'utem'.

i Note that if you click on the **AutoCorrect** button in the Spelling and Grammar dialog box Word will add your mistake and the selected change to the AutoCorrect list.

Using the thesaurus

The thesaurus can be used to add variety and interest to your work. A thesaurus finds synonyms and related words. The thesaurus is used for one word at a time. Place the insertion point in the appropriate word and then choose **Tools-Language-Thesaurus** (shortcut key *Shift/F7*). The Thesaurus dialog box appears.

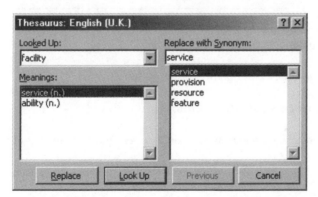

The word that was selected appears in the **Looked Up** box. Underneath this is the **Meanings** box, which lists related words and indicates whether these words are nouns or verbs. Next to the **Looked Up** box is a **Replace with Synonym** box, which contains a list of synonyms for the selected word. You can replace the selected word with any of the words listed by clicking on the word. It will then appear in the text box at the top of the list and clicking on the **Replace** button will put it into the document in place of the word selected.

If the list of synonyms is not extensive enough then the thesaurus can be used to find synonyms for the word in the **Looked Up** box. To do this, click on the **Look Up** button. This may be repeated until a suitable synonym is found.

The thesaurus keeps a list of all the words you have looked up. To return to a previous word open the **Looked Up** list box by clicking on the arrow at the end of the box. Words that you have previously looked up are displayed and the required word can be chosen from the list.

Task 6: Using the thesaurus

Key the following text into a new document and save it as *Promote*.

Chelmer Leisure and Recreation Centre has a small promotional budget with which the management can use as they see fit. In the event of a new fitness suite being opened at the centre a great deal of effort must be channelled into creating awareness of the new facility to the potential customer.

The centre is a local authority facility which opens up a range of areas for promotional activities. Other local amenities provide excellent space to promote the new facility. Libraries, other sports facilities, Town Halls and Theatres are venues where any promotional material advertising the new facility can be placed.

Local papers are an excellent promotional tool in the area. There are two popular local papers which are issued weekly and circulated throughout the area. These are the Herald, which is sold throughout the Borough and the Advertiser which is a free newspaper.

Using the Thesaurus investigate synonyms for the following words: deal, creating, range, popular.

1. Place the insertion point in the word to be investigated.

2. Select **Tools-Language-Thesaurus**.

3. Consider whether a replacement should be selected from the list of synonyms.

4. Investigate the effect of 'looking up' a word. Remember that a list of words looked up can be viewed by opening the **Looked Up** list box.

Using AutoText

The activities described in this section are aimed at reducing the amount of keying that might be performed in producing a document.

Creating AutoText entries

Word uses AutoText to save repeated keying of the same text. Some documents contain text (and/or graphics) which is repeated several or many times. For example, a company name, address or logo may appear several times in one document or may be required in many documents. By defining the name, address or logo as an AutoText entry it may be recalled at any point in any document with a simple keying action. To take a simple example, the text 'Yours sincerely' appears at the end of many business letters. If several letters are to be typed then defining this as an AutoText entry would help to save time keying.

Word maintains a list of AutoText entries, which you can add to or delete from. An AutoText entry may be text, graphics or a mixture of text and graphics. You can save any text or graphics that you use often as an AutoText entry; then you can easily insert the text or graphics into a document with a simple keying action, rather than retyping or using copy and paste.

Making an AutoText entry

First type in the text that you intend to make into an AutoText entry. Check the spelling is correct and select the text. Choose **Insert-AutoText-AutoText** and the AutoCorrect dialog box appears.

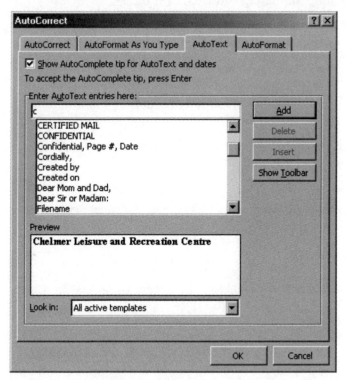

In the **Enter AutoText entries here** box type a name for the AutoText entry: in this example, 'c' for 'Chelmer Leisure and Recreation Centre'. Then click on the **Add** button.

Using an AutoText entry

The simplest method of using an AutoText entry is to type the AutoText name followed immediately by *F3*, i.e. typing **c** and pressing *F3* would produce the text 'Chelmer Leisure and Recreation Centre'.

Alternatively, if you forget your AutoText names (for example, *ys* could be the glossary name for 'Yours sincerely') then use Insert-AutoText. In the dialog box will be a list of your previously defined AutoText entries. Type or select the AutoText name you wish to use and click on the **Insert** button.

AutoText prompts

You may have noticed that as you begin to type some words – for example, days of the week – Word prompts you with the completed word or phase. This is another way in which AutoText works. If instead of using *c* as the AutoText name for 'Chelmer Leisure and Recreation Centre' the full text was used as the name then as you began to type **Chelmer** you would be prompted with the full text. You may have both names defined so that you can either use *c/F3* or expect to be prompted each time you type **Chelmer**.

Task 7: Creating and using AutoText entries

Open a new document and try setting up and using the following AutoText entries:

AutoText name	AutoText entry
ys	Yours sincerely
yf	Yours faithfully

1. Type out the AutoText entry in full, e.g. **Yours sincerely**.

2. Select this text.

3. Use **Insert-AutoText** and in the **Enter AutoText entries here** box type the AutoText name, e.g. **ys**.

4. Click on **Add**.

5. Move the insertion point to a place where the AutoText entry is to appear.

6. Type the AutoText name, e.g. **ys**, and press *F3*.

7. Type out the second AutoText entry in full, e.g. **Yours faithfully**.

8. Select this text. Use **Insert-AutoText**; accept *Yours faithfully* as the name for the AutoText entry and click on **Add**.

9.   Start typing **Yours faithfully** and you should be prompted when you reach the **f** of **faithfully**; press <u>Enter</u> to accept the prompt.

Experiment with creating other AutoText entries. Do not save this document.

Task 8: Editing an AutoText entry

Add the following paragraph to the document *Promote* created earlier in Task 6.

This form of advertising, i.e. posters, advertisements in local papers, offers a direct link with the public. The money that is spent now to promote the new fitness suite is done so in the hope of increasing usage. The outcome of this form of promotion is uncertain but the main aims are to:

- create awareness of the new fitness suite

- inform the public of the services on offer at the centre

- educate/inform of the benefits of the new fitness suite.

---

1.   After typing **new fitness suite** select it.

2.   Use **Insert-AutoText** to define it as an AutoText entry with the name *n*.

3.   Next time this needs to be keyed in simply type *n* followed by <u>F3</u>.

Mail Merging

What you will learn in this unit

This unit shows you how to create a series of personalised documents, all based on a single document. At the end of this unit you will be able to:

❑ Create a standard letter.

❑ Create a set of data.

❑ Perform a mail merge.

Mail merging

The word 'mailshot' is commonly used in the business environment. It means to send out many duplicated letters to a target audience, often for advertising or market research. A word processor's mail merge facility can 'personalise' a standard letter so that, for example, the recipient's name and address are printed. This unit explains how to use Word to perform a simple mail merge.

Two documents are required for a mail merge:

❑ The *standard letter*. This contains the standard text plus areas that are marked as 'replaceable', i.e. personal information can be slotted into them.

❑ The *data document*. This is a document containing the personal information that is to be slotted into the standard letter. Each person's information is in a separate paragraph.

First make a plan of the standard letter to decide which information is to be replaceable, for example a name, company, street, town, county and postcode. Then create a list of data to insert in the document. It is simplest to create both of these documents in the same directory. Finally, perform the mail merge. Word will help you through these three stages of mail merging.

Task 1: Mail merging

The first stage is to create the standard letter (the main document).

1. Open a new document.

2. Key in the address of the centre as follows:

Chelmer Leisure and Recreation Centre
Park View Road
Chelmer
Cheshire
CE9 5JS
12th October 2001

3. Save the document as *Mail*.

4. Choose **Tools-Mail Merge-Options**. The Mail Merge Helper dialog box appears.

5. Click on the **Create** button. Choose **Form Letters**. The active window, *Mail*, becomes the basis for the form letters.

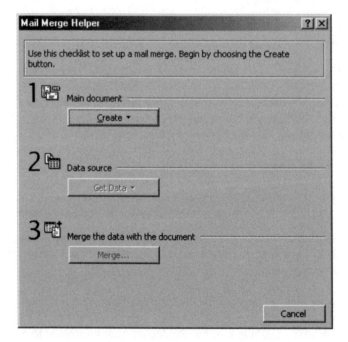

The next step is to specify the data source or to create the data source.

6. Click on the **Get Data** button. Choose **Create Data Source**. The Create Dala Source dialog box is displayed. In this box you define the names of your replaceable fields.

7. Click on *FirstName* (in the **Field names in header row** box) and click on the **Remove Field Name** button. Repeat for all fields except *Title*, *LastName*, *Company* and *PostalCode*.

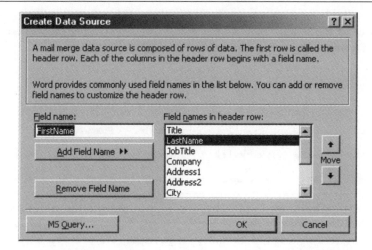

8. Type **Street** into the **Field name** box and click on **Add Field Name**. Repeat for **Town** and again for **County**. Use the 'Move' arrow buttons to reorder the field headers so that they are in the order *Title, LastName, Company, Street, Town, County* and *PostalCode*.

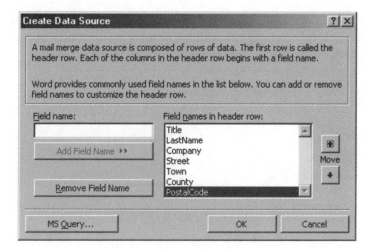

9. Click on **OK**. Save your data source as *Supplier*.

10. You are warned that there are no data records in the file. Choose **Edit Data Source**.

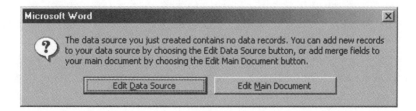

11. A table for entering data records is displayed. Enter the following records. (**Hint**: use the *Tab* key to move from one box to the next. After each record is entered click on the *Tab* key to create a new row.

Title	LastName	Company	Street	Town	County	PostalCode
Mrs	Allen	Medlock Leisure Centre	Fold Avenue	Droylsen	Tameside	DRl7 5TG
Mr	Royle	Universal Gym (Europe) Ltd	Hutton	Brentwood	Essex	CMl3 1XA
Mr	Bradbury	Atlanta Sports Industries Ltd	Atlanta House	Maltby	Rotherham	S66 8QN
Miss	Jackson	Physique Training Equipment Ltd	Bankfield Mill	Colne	Lancashire	BB8 9PD

12. When the last record is complete, close and save the file as *Supplier*. You will return to the letter document. Notice that there is an extra toolbar for mail merging. This toolbar can be moved by dragging the vertical bar on the left-hand side.

13. If you wish to edit your data file, open and edit the *Supplier* file. To change the data source, click on the  (**Mail Merge Helper**) button; otherwise, carry on to the next step, which adds to the document as shown below.

Chelmer Leisure and Recreation Centre
Park View Road
Chelmer
Cheshire
CE9 5JS
12th October 2001

«Company»
«Street»
«Town»
«County»
«PostalCode»

Dear «Title» «LastName»

Thank you for your interest in providing equipment for our new fitness suite. Please could you submit a formal quote for our consideration.

Yours sincerely

G. V. Richards
Manager

14. Position the insertion point for the first line of the company address below the date. Click on the **Insert Merge Field** button to display a drop-down list of the fields in the data file.

15. Click on *Company*.

16. Press *Enter* for the next line of the address, click on the **Insert Merge Field** button and highlight *Street*. Build up the address and greeting as shown below. Remember to insert a space between the *Title* field and the *LastName* field.

17. Save these additions to the document *Mail*.

18. You may wish to click on the  (**Check for Errors**) button in the Mail Merge toolbar to check the data file. The most common error is where the number of fields in a record does not correspond with the number of fields that have been specified. Choose the option **Simulate the merge and report errors in a new document**.

19. Click on the ▣ (**Merge to Printer**) button in the Mail Merge toolbar to print the merged letters. One letter will be produced for each record of data.

20. If you wish to merge the letters to a file rather than printing them, this can be done by clicking on the ▣ (**Merge to New Document**) button on the Mail Merge toolbar. Each letter in the new document will be separated from the next by a section break. Don't forget to save this new document if you wish to keep the merge for later printing.

21. Close the Mail Merge toolbar.

Printing envelopes and labels

As well as producing the merged letters Word provides a facility to print envelopes or labels by merging an address list. These two facilities will be explored in the following tasks.

Task 2: Printing envelopes

1. With the standard letter created in the last task still open, choose **Tools-Mail Merge-Options**.

2. Click on the **Create** button and choose **Envelopes**. Next choose **New Main Document**.

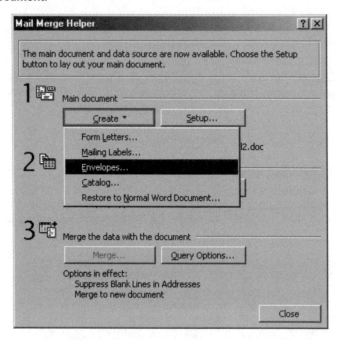

3. Click on the **Get Data** button. Next click on **Open Data Source**, and select the directory of the file *Supplier.doc*. Click on **Open** after highlighting this file. Next click on **Setup** in the **Main Document** section.

4. On the **Envelope Options** tab, select the envelope size you want, and adjust the address format and position on the envelope.

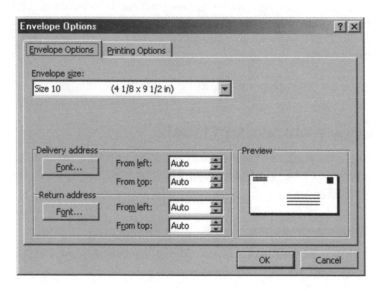

5. On the **Printing Options** tab, make sure that the selected envelope feed options are correct for your printer, and then click on **OK**.

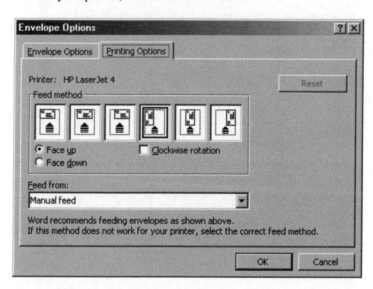

6. In the **Envelope Address** dialog box, insert the merge fields for the address information as shown below.

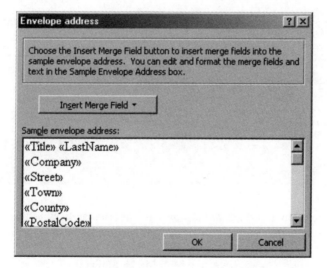

7. Click on **OK** and you will be returned to the Mail Merge Helper dialog box. Click on the **Merge** button.

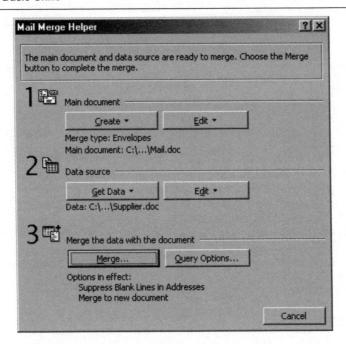

8. In the **Merge To** box choose **New Document** or **Printer**. If you choose **Printer**, the envelopes will be printed straight away; choosing **New Document** will allow for later printing. Click on **Merge**.

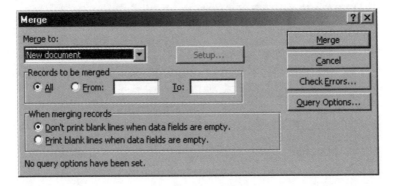

 Note: It is possible to print envelopes only for selected addressees by clicking on **Query Options** and then specifying criteria for selecting the data records.

9. Save the file as Envelopes. Close the Mail Merge toolbar.

Task 3: Printing labels

The steps to printing labels are essentially the same as those for printing envelopes. In the second step choose **Mailing labels** and in step 4 select the type of labels you require.

Inserting Symbols, Codes and Equations

What you will learn in this unit

This unit concentrates on specialised symbols and equations. At the end of this unit you will be able to:

❑ Enter special characters in foreign words.

❑ Create simple mathematical and scientific formulae.

Other slightly more advanced techniques that can be used in document creation will be examined in this unit. This unit also introduces the equation editor and shows you how to add complex formulae to your documents.

You will be able to:

❑ Use fields.

❑ Apply multi-level bullets.

❑ Use the Equation Editor.

What you need

To complete this unit you will need:

❑ The document file *Appointment Memo* created in Unit 4.

❑ The document file *Health Suite Times* created in Unit 7.

Scientific, mathematical and foreign symbols

For normal work the letters and symbols that appear on the keyboard are sufficient. However, there may be occasions where a foreign word containing symbols that are not in the English alphabet needs to be included. Another area in which non-standard letters are required is in the production of a scientific or mathematical document.

For mathematical use, the Windows Symbol font contains the Greek alphabet and a variety of mathematical symbols. There are foreign characters in most of the 'normal' fonts (Arial, Times etc.)

To insert a symbol or foreign letter:

1. Position the insertion point where the character is to appear.

2. Use **Insert-Symbol**. The Symbol dialog box appears. Select the **Symbols** tab.

3. Open the dropdown **Font** list box, select the particular font required and all the symbols available in that font will be displayed in a matrix. For foreign text choose *(normal text)*, for mathematical symbols choose *Symbol* and for fun characters choose *Wingdings*.

4. A symbol is selected using the pointer by pointing and clicking. The chosen symbol is displayed in a larger size as white text on a blue background (default colours).

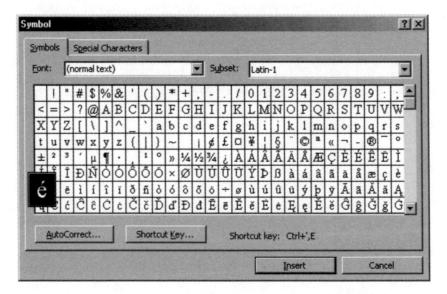

5. To insert the symbol into the document, click on **Insert**. The symbol will take the current point size that is being used. Close the Symbol dialog box by clicking on the **Close** button if you have inserted a symbol or **Cancel** if you have not.

Task 1: Using scientific, mathematical and foreign symbols

Start a new document, and, selecting symbols from *(normal text)* and *Symbol*, key in the following:

Fête   café Σx $a \geq b$ 100°C

Defining foreign language portions of a document

If a portion of a document, or indeed all of it, is to be written in a foreign language then Word needs to be made aware of this. You will not want Word to spell check a paragraph in, say, French using an English dictionary. If French proofing tools (spelling and grammar) are available these are used instead.

To format text as being in a foreign language:

1. Select the text.

2. Choose **Tools-Language-Set Language** and in the dialog box select the language required. Click on **OK**.

Using fields

Fields are instructions to Word to perform a certain task. You will probably have inserted fields into a document without realising it.

Fields can be quite complicated and it is not the intention to go into very much detail on this subject. Therefore only two types of fields will be considered. These are the date field and sequence numbering fields. Having a flavour of these may encourage you to experiment with other field types.

Task 2: Using a date field

A date field is particularly useful in a standard letter or memo template. This exercise will insert an updateable date field into the file *Appointment Memo* created in Task 2 of Unit 4. Open the file.

1. Position the insertion point at the place where the date is to go. Delete the existing date.

2. Choose **Insert-Date and Time**.

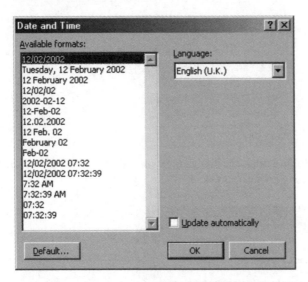

3. Select the format of the date from the **Date and Time** box.

4. Check the **Update automatically** box. This will insert the date as a field. Click on **OK**.

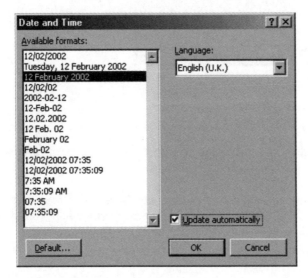

5. Select **Tools-Options**, click on the **View** tab and under **Show** tick the **Field codes** check box. Click on **OK**.

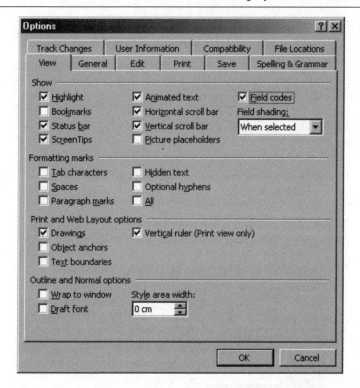

You should see the numbers change into their underlying formulas, enclosed in curly brackets. These are codes which are instructions to Word to perform the calculation.

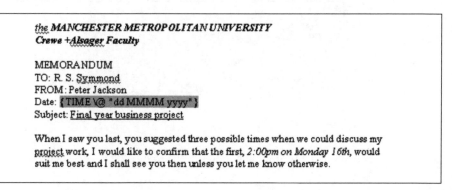

6. Use **Tools-Options** again to change back to the usual view by removing the tick from the **Field codes** check box.

7. The date field will not automatically update so that if you were to open the memo in a few days time the date would still be that of when the field was created. To update the field select the date and press *F9*.

Using fields to sequence numbers

The sequence number field type is useful if you have a numbering sequence for chapters, sections, paragraphs, figures, tables etc. in your document. It saves having to check back through the document to see what the last number in the sequence was. To insert a sequence field:

1. Position the insertion point at the place in the document where the number is to go.

2. Choose **Insert-Field**, then select **Numbering** from **Categories** and **Seq** from **Field names**.

3. Click in the **Field codes** box after **Seq** and type the name of the sequence of numbers, e.g. *table* for a sequence of numbers for tables. Click on **OK**.

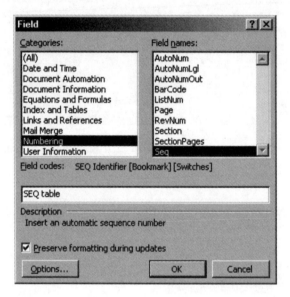

Alternatively:

1. Position the insertion point at the place in the document where the number is to go.

2. Press *Ctrl+F9* and inside the curly brackets (which are not ordinary curly brackets) type **seq table**.

3. Press *F9*.

This kind of field code may be viewed individually by positioning the insertion point in the field, clicking the right mouse button and selecting **Toggle Field Codes**. The same command redisplays the field value.

This shortcut menu also offers an alternative way of updating the field by choosing **Update Field**.

Note that care must be taken to ensure that the fields are updated. For example, a table might be added or removed from the document. Fields may be updated individually as described for the date field or in the case of a sequence the whole document can be selected and all fields updated by pressing *F9*.

Task 3: Sequencing fields

This task adds table numbers to the *Health Suite Times* document from Unit 7.

1. Open the *Health Suite Times* document.

2. Below each table:

    ❏   Insert a blank line.

    ❏   Type *Table* and a space.

    ❏   Press *Ctrl+F9*. Shaded curly brackets appear.

    ❏   Inside the curly brackets type ***seq table***.

    ❏   Press *F9* to turn the field into a number.

```
Saturday    9.00am - 1.00pm        Men Only
            1.00pm - 5.00pm        Mixed
Sunday      9.00am - 5.00pm        Mixed
Table { seq table }
```

3. Save the document.

Multi-level bullets

As well as creating straightforward bulleted and numbered lists, Word also allows you to create lists within lists, known as *multi-level lists*. The following task illustrates the creation of a multi-level list.

Task 4: Multi-level lists

1. Type in the list below as a bulleted list without the indents and using standard bullets.

2. Select the entire list and choose **Format-Bullets and Numbering**.

❖ Fitness Suite

➤ Super Circuit Training

➤ Personalised Exercise Programmes

❖ Health Suite

➤ Sauna and Steam Room

➤ Power Shower

➤ Jacuzzi Relaxation Lounge

➤ Sunbeds

3. Click on the **Outline Numbered** tab and select the multi-level bullets. Click on **OK**.

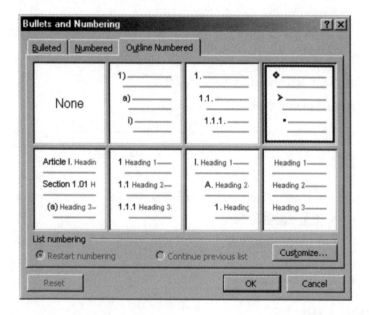

4. Position the insertion point in the second point and click on the 🔢 (**Increase Indent**) button on the formatting toolbar. Repeat for the other indented points.

5. You can modify the bullets by selecting the whole text again and choosing **Format-Bullets and Numbering**. Choose **Customize**. In the **Level** box select level 2 (see below).

6. Open the **Number style** list box. Scroll down to **New Bullet**. In the Symbol dialog box select a font and choose a symbol for the bullet. Click on **OK**.

7. Experiment with adding additional points and selecting their level using the buttons.

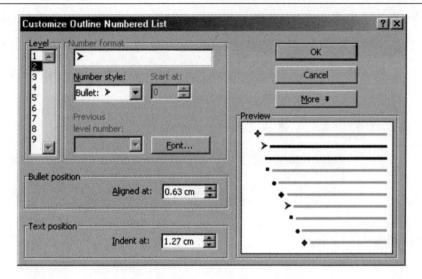

8. Try using numbers and a combination of numbers and bullets in a multi-level list. You will find Word provides a selection of choices in the **Outline Numbered gallery.**

The Equation Editor

One of the most difficult tasks in word processing is to write an equation, particularly if the equation has a complicated structure. Lining up numerator and denominator, positioning brackets, using subscripts and superscripts, to name but a few, are typical of the problems encountered when constructing an equation. Word provides a means to overcome this in the form of an Equation Editor. The Equation Editor will not be examined in detail; however, the basics will be covered.

The equation is constructed using Equation Editor toolbars and is then embedded into the document by clicking outside the equation. The equation may be edited by double-clicking on it.

Starting the Equation Editor

The Equation Editor is available through the **Insert-Object** command. From the Object dialog box choose **Microsoft Equation 3.0**. Click on **OK** to select this option. Notice that other 'objects' can be activated through this dialog box. If this object is not available then you will be given the opportunity to install it.

The Equation Editor floating toolbar should appear, along with the equation editing work space. Note that only the menu bar and ruler remain at the top of the screen.

The Equation Editor toolbars

The Equation Editor toolbar is composed of two palettes, the symbol palette and the template palette. The insertion point looks different; it is flashing vertical and horizontal lines inside a dotted rectangle, in the equation editing workspace, known as a slot.

Building an equation

It is best to write down the equation to be created so that its method of construction can be considered. The basic rule for creating an equation is to set up a template first and then fill the slots in the template with symbols. If the wrong template is inserted by mistake use **Edit-Undo** to remove it.

Templates are chosen from the lower palette bar. The icons in this bar represent the categories of template. By clicking and holding the mouse button on one of these icons a sub-menu appears showing all the templates available in that category. Still holding the mouse button down, move to the one required and release the button. Symbols can be inserted into the template to complete the equation.

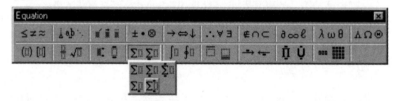

It is beyond the scope of this unit to go into very much detail concerning equation creation. However, by illustrating the creation of some basic statistical equations encountered by business students, it is hoped to provide a firm base from which to explore the capabilities of the Equation Editor.

Task 5: Creating an equation for the mean of grouped data

The equation to be produced is that for calculating the mean value of a set of grouped data.

$$\bar{x} = \frac{\sum fx_{mid}}{\sum f}$$

1. Start a new document. Position the insertion point at the place where the equation is to be and use **Insert-Object-Microsoft Equation 3.0**.

2. Type **x**. Click on the third icon on the symbols bar. Click on the first box in the fourth row.

3. Type **=**. It is worth noting at this point that you cannot type a space into an equation; the editor sorts out the spacing.

4. Click on the second icon on the template bar. Click on the first box in the first row.

5. Click on the fourth icon on the template bar. Click on the first box in the first row.

6. Type **fx**.

7. Click on the third icon on the template bar. Click on the second box in the first row.

8. Type **mid**.

9. Click on the denominator part of the equation.

10. Using a template, insert a Σ as for the numerator.

11. Type **f**. Click outside the working area to embed the equation in the document.

12. Save the document as *Stats*.

Task 6: Creating an equation for standard deviation

Keeping open the document just created, on a new line create the following equation for the standard deviation of ungrouped data.

$$\sigma = \sqrt{\frac{\sum (x - \bar{x})^2}{n}}$$

1. Position the insertion point at the place where the equation is to be and use **Insert-Object-Microsoft Equation 3.0**.

2. Click on the ninth icon on the symbols bar. Click on the letter that is first on the sixth row. Type **=**.

3. Click on the second icon on the template bar. Click on the first box in the fourth row.

4. Click on the second icon on the template bar. Click on the first box in the first row.

5. Click on the fourth icon on the template bar. Click on the first box in the first row.

6. Click on the first icon on the template bar. Click on the first box in the first row.

7. Type **x-x**.

8. Click on the third icon on the symbols bar. Click on the first box in the fourth row.

9. Press the right arrow button to move the insertion point to the end of the brackets.

10. Click on the third icon on the template bar. Click on the first box in the first row. Type **2**.

11. Click on the denominator slot. Make sure the insertion point is flashing in this slot.

12. Type **n**. Click outside the working area to embed the equation in the document.

13. Save the document.

Task 7: Creating the equation for the gradient of a line of best fit

Finally, add the equation to find the gradient of a line of best fit.

$$m = \dfrac{\sum xy - \dfrac{\sum x \sum y}{n}}{\sum x^2 - \dfrac{\left(\sum x\right)^2}{n}}$$

1. Position the insertion point at the place where the equation is to be and use **Insert-Object-Microsoft Equation 3.0**.

2. Type **m=**. Click on the second icon on the template bar. Click on the first box in the first row.

3. Click on the fourth icon on the template bar. Click on the first box in the first row. Type **xy-**.

4. Click on the second icon on the template bar. Click on the first box in the first row.

5. Click on the fourth icon on the template bar. Click on the first box in the first row. Type **x**.

6. Click on the fourth icon on the template bar. Click on the first box in the first row. Type **y**.

7. Click in the denominator slot of this part and type *n*.

8. Click in the main denominator slot to move the insertion point into it.

9. Click on the fourth icon on the template bar. Click on the first box in the first row. Type *x*.

10. Click on the third icon on the template bar. Click on the first box in the first row. Type **2**.

11. Press the down arrow button and type -.

12. Click on the second icon on the template bar. Click on the first box in the first row.

13. Click on the first icon on the template bar. Click on the first box in the first row.

14. Click on the fourth icon on the template bar. Click on the first box in the first row. Type *x* and press the right arrow button twice to move the insertion point to the end of the brackets.

15. Click on the third icon on the template bar. Click on the first box in the first row. Type **2**.

16. Click in the denominator slot.

17. Type *n*. Embed the equation in the document. Save.

Adjusting settings in the Equation Editor

To make adjustments to the font and size of an equation use either **Style-Define** or **Size-Define**. **Style-Define** will allow different fonts to be applied and **Size-Define** will allow the size of the individual parts that make up an equation to be altered.

Creating Tables

What you will learn in this unit

This unit explains how to create tables of text. The tables feature is a more sophisticated way of creating the tables that you set up in Unit 7 with tab stops. Tables created with the tables feature are easy to format. Unit 17 shows you how to create forms using tables and Unit 18 goes on to demonstrate how borders and shading can be applied to tables. At the end of this unit you will be able to:

❏ Set up a simple table.

❏ Enter text in a table.

❏ Select text in a table and perform simple formatting operations.

❏ Sort text in a table.

❏ Perform simple calculations in a table.

Tables are an easy way to arrange and adjust columns of text and numbers, and are much more flexible than tabs. Once you have taken a few moments to master tables you will wonder how you ever managed without them. A table can be inserted at any point in your text. A table offers an easy way to group paragraphs side by side and to arrange text beside related graphics on a page. Tables can be used to organise information in the data documents that are merged to create form letters, mailing labels and other merged documents. By adding borders and shading to a table you can create many types of forms. Tables allow easy transfer of data between Excel and Word. If you create a table in Word, you can insert the table in an Excel worksheet and work with it as you would with any other spreadsheet data; the converse is also possible. Insert an Excel worksheet into a Word document and you can work with the data just as you would with a Word table. However, more of these ambitious applications of tables later.

Setting up a simple table

To set up a table:

1. Position the insertion point where you want to insert the table.

2. Click on the ▦ button on the toolbar. (If you can't see the button, click on ⯈ to display more buttons.)

3. On the grid, drag the pointer to select the number of columns and rows that you want the new table to have.

4. Release the mouse button to insert the table.

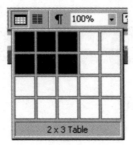

Alternatively:

1. Select **Table-Insert-Table**.

2. In the **Number of Columns** box, type or select a number indicating how many columns you want.

3. Click on **OK**.

Or:

1. Choose **Table-Draw Table**. Drag the drawing tool to create the outside box of the table. Release the mouse button.

2. Drag the drawing tool to draw in vertical and horizontal lines to complete the grid for this table.

Note: You can add rows and adjust column widths later to suit your needs. It is usually a good idea to accept the defaults on your first try.

Entering text in a table

Once you have created a table, you should have an empty grid, with the insertion point in the first cell so that you can start typing. Mostly you can move the insertion point and select and edit text in the same way as in the rest of your document. As you enter text the boxes will expand to accommodate it.

To	Operation
Start new paragraphs in a cell	Press *Enter*.
Move to the next cell	Press *Tab*.
Move to the first cell in the next row	Press *Tab* in the rightmost cell.
Add another row of cells	Press *Tab* in the last cell in the table.
Leave the table	Place the insertion point after the table before typing.
Insert a tab stop	With the pointer in the box in which you wish to insert a tab stop, click on the [L] button to select the type of tab stop, then, while depressing *Ctrl*, click on the ruler where you wish to insert the tab stop.
Change the column width	Drag the cell border of the column whose width you want to change.

Task 1: Creating a table

1. Open a new document.

2. Create a table either by using the **Table-Insert Table** command or the ▦ button, with three columns and one row.

3. Type in the heading in the first cell. Press *Tab* three times to add a row.

How much fat is the limit?		
Type of fat	Saturated	Other fats
12.5st (80kg) man		
Inactive	28g	68g
Quite active	35g	82g
Very active	42g	97g
9.5st (61kg) woman		
Inactive	22g	51g
Quite active	27g	63g
Very active	31g	74g

4. Enter the text into the columns, moving between columns using the _Tab_ key. Also use the _Tab_ key to create each new row in the table. If you need to adjust the width of the columns do so by dragging the column boundary. Do not try to format the column headings yet.

5. The table as displayed has borders. Remove these by selecting **Format-Borders and Shading**, and then clicking on **None**, followed by **OK**. This leaves grey grid-lines, which will not be printed.

6. Save the document as _Fat Limit_ and close it.

Note: When you create a table (with the borders switched off), Word displays _grid-lines_ between cells. These help you to see which cell you are working in. These can be hidden by choosing **Table-Hide Gridlines**. It is usually best to work with the gridlines on. Gridlines will not be printed.

Selecting within a table

In order to edit, format or add a border to certain parts of a table it is necessary to select specific parts of the table. Remember that the selected area will be high-lighted in black. Selection can be achieved as indicated below.

To select	Operation
Cell	Click in the cell's selection area, which is a strip down its left side where the mouse pointer changes to a right-pointing arrow.
Any rectangular area of cells	Place the mouse pointer anywhere in the top left cell and drag down and to the right until the area you want is selected.
Row	Click in the row selection bar to the left of the row, or double click in any cell's selection area in the row. Alternatively, choose **Table-Select Row**.
Column	Click in the column selection bar at the top of the column, or click anywhere in the column with the right mouse button. Alternatively, choose **Table-Select Column**.
Whole table	Point to the leftmost column, hold down the right mouse button, and drag across the table. Alternatively, choose **Table-Select Table**.

Once you have selected text within a table it is possible to apply formatting, moving, copying and other operations to text in the same way as with text elsewhere in the document. For example, with appropriate cells selected, the following operations may be performed.

To	Do this
Delete	Choose **Edit-Cut**.
Copy	Choose **Edit-Copy** or **Edit-Cut**. Move the insertion point and choose **Edit-Paste**.
Display the headings in each column in bold	Select the first row of the table, containing the headings, and click on the **B** button.
Align text within a cell	Set tab stops.
Adjust the alignment of paragraphs within cells	Click on the alignment formatting buttons.
Move a row of cells	Select the row. Position the mouse pointer at the beginning of the selected row, drag the selected row to the new location, then release the left mouse button.
Sort a table on the basis of the contents in a given column	Select the sort column. Choose **Table-Sort**. The Sort dialog box will be displayed. Select the appropriate column and then for **Type** choose **Text**. Select an ascending or a descending sort. Click on **OK**. Rows are ordered alphabetically according to the text in the sorted column.

Task 2: Formatting a table

Open the document *Fat Limit*. Format the column headings by first selecting them and then applying appropriate formatting (see example below).

1. To select the first cell, click on its left side.

2. Click on the **B** and *I* buttons to format the text.

3. Repeat this operation with the other cells whose text requires formatting.

How much fat is the limit?		
Type of fat	*Saturated*	*Other fats*
12.5st (80kg) man		
Inactive	28g	68g
Quite active	35g	82g
Very active	42g	97g
9.5st (61kg) woman		
Inactive	22g	51g
Quite active	27g	63g
Very active	31g	74g

4. Select the whole table and use **Format-Paragraph** to set the space before and after each line to 3 points.

5. Increase the spacing above the two sub-headings.

6. Save the file.

Task 3: Sorting a table and adding rows

In a new document:

1. Insert a table with three columns and one row using **Table-Insert Table**.

2. Adjust the column widths by dragging them to accommodate the addresses shown below.

Supplier	Address	Telephone
Universal Gym (Europe) Ltd	Hutton, Brentwood, Essex CM13 1XA	01277 221122
Atlanta Sports Industries Ltd	Atlanta House, Rotherway, Euroway Estate, Maltby, Rotherham, S66 8QN	01709 700555
Physique Training Equipment Ltd	Bankfield Mill, Greenfield, Road, Come, Lancashire, BB8 9PD	01282 863300

3. Insert the names, addresses and telephone numbers (not the column headings) into the cells.

4. Sort the table on the basis of the contents of the Supplier column, by selecting that column, and choosing **Table-Sort** and appropriate options from the Sort dialog box. Click on **OK**. Rows should be ordered alphabetically according to the text in the sorted column.

5. To add a row for column headings place the pointer in the top left-hand corner and use **Table-Insert Rows**.

6. Enter the text of the column headings (in bold).

7. Save the document as *Address*.

Calculations

Basic mathematical calculations can be performed within a Word document. Word allows figures to be added, subtracted, multiplied and divided. Word assumes that you will perform calculations in a table, in a manner similar to using a spreadsheet. It also offers some spreadsheet formatting and functions, such as MAX, MIN and AVERAGE.

Adding figures in a table

Often figures that are presented in a tabular form are totalled and the **Table-Formula** command can be used for this purpose. The task below illustrates this process. (An alternative to this method is to display the Tables and Borders toolbar, and with the insertion point in the destination cell click on the **AutoSum** button.)

Task 4: Performing calculations in a table

Into a new document, key in the following table:

Adult	140
Junior	20
Concessionary	70
Club Adult	20
Club junior	10
Total	

1. Position the insertion point in the cell in the table where the answer is to appear, i.e. the empty cell opposite *Total*.

2. Choose **Table-Formula**. A Formula dialog box appears in which Word proposes a formula, in this case *=SUM(ABOVE)*, which means it will total the column above the cell selected. Click on **OK** and the answer, 260, will be inserted into the table.

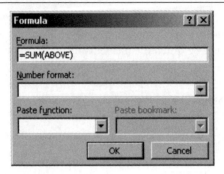

3. Close the document without saving.

Formulae

Task 4 showed how a column of figures in text could be totalled using a simple equation. You can include more sophisticated calculations in tables.

Task 5: Simple formulae

Start a new document. Enter the following table with which some simple formulae will be used.

3	4	
6	2	

1. Position the insertion point in the empty cell at the top of the third column.

2. Choose **Table-Formula**. A Formula dialog box appears in which the proposed formula is =SUM(LEFT) which means it will total the row to the left of the selected cell. Click on **OK** and the answer, 7, will be inserted into the table.

3. Imagine that each column in the table is denoted by a letter of the alphabet (so in the table above there are columns A, B and C) and that each row in the table is denoted by a number (rows 1, 2 and 3). Each cell in the table can be uniquely identified by its 'grid reference', i.e. the top left cell is A1 and the bottom right cell is C3. If you have used a spreadsheet you will be familiar with this concept.

   Position the insertion point in cell C2. Use **Table-Formula** and edit the proposed formula so that it reads **=A2*B2**. Click on **OK**. The * means multiply. Is the answer what you expected?

4. Position the insertion point in cell A3. Use Table-Formula and edit the proposed formula so that it reads **=C2/A1** instead. Click on **OK**. The / means divide.

5. Position the insertion point in cell B3. Use **Table-Formula** and edit the proposed formula so that it reads *=C2–C1* instead. Click on **OK**. The – means subtract.

6. Position the insertion point in cell C3. Use **Table-Formula** and edit the proposed formula so that it reads *=SUM(A1 :C2)* instead. Click on **OK**. The result is the sum of all the values in the specified range. A range is a rectangle of cells, identified by the top left (A1 in this case) and bottom right (C2) cells: i.e. A1, A2, B1, B2, C1 and C2 in this example.

3	4	7
6	2	12
4	5	34

7. Close the document without saving it.

Unit 17

Creating Forms

What you will learn in this unit

This unit continues the theme of Unit 16, the use of tables. It introduces some more sophisticated editing features and demonstrates how tables can be used to create forms and other more complex documents. At the end of this unit you will be able to:

❑ Format a table by, for instance, inserting and deleting rows.

❑ Use table formatting to create a simple form.

❑ Put existing text into a table.

What you need

To complete this unit you will need:

❑ The document file *Health Suite Times* created in Unit 7.

Editing a table

As you develop a table you will find that you may need to insert or delete a row or column, delete or insert single cells, or split a table into two separate tables. This may be achieved as shown in the following table.

To	Do this
Insert a row	Select the row below where you want to insert a new row and select **Table-Insert-Rows Above**. To insert a new row at the bottom of the table place the cursor below the last row of the table and choose **Table-Insert-Rows Above**; alternatively, place the cursor in the right-most cell of the last row and press *Tab*.
Insert a column	Select the column to the right of where you wish to add the new column and select **Table-Insert-Columns to the Left**. To enter a column to the right of the table, place the cursor in the last column and choose **Table-Insert-Columns to the Right**.
Delete a row	Select the row or rows and choose **Table-Delete-Rows**.

Delete a column	Select the column or columns and choose **Table-Delete-Columns**.
Insert a single cell	Select a cell and choose **Table-Insert-Cells**. Decide where to shift the displaced cells: i.e. to either to the right on the row or down the column. Choose either **Insert Entire Row** or **Insert Entire Column**, if you are accidentally using the wrong command.

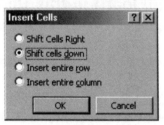

Delete a single cell	Proceed as for inserting a single cell, choosing whether to close up the row or column.
Split a table into two separate tables	Select the row that is to become the top row of the second table and choose **Table-Split Table**. A normal paragraph will be inserted to break the table into two parts. This command offers a way of inserting normal text above a table at the start of a document.
Split a cell into two cells	Select the cell, and choose **Table-Split Cells**. In the Split Cells dialog box choose the number of columns (or rows). Click on **OK**. Cells can be merged in a similar way using **Table-Merge Cells**.

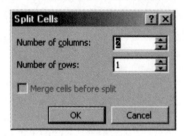

Task 1: Editing a table

This task asks you to use some of the formatting skills that you have learnt when using tables to design a form. There are a number of tips for form design:

❑ Remember the form's purpose, and keep the gaps the right size.

❑ Leave bigger gaps for manual filling.

❑ Request all necessary information but no unnecessary information.

❑ Ask for information in a logical sequence.

❏ Make sure the headings are clear and designed to help the reader to understand the form.

Taking all of these points into consideration, we wish to design a form for application for membership for a Health and Fitness Club, which looks something like the one shown below, but which may be formatted slightly differently if you choose.

Chelmer Leisure and Recreation Centre			
Health and Fitness Club			
Membership Application Form			
Name			
Address			
		Telephone	
Occupation		Date of Birth	
Sporting		Date of Joining	
Interests			
For Office Use Only			
Date Subs Due		Subs Paid	Mem.Cat

1. Type in the first three rows.

2. Justify and format these three rows.

3. Insert a table with four columns using **Table-Insert Table**.

4. Start to enter the labels. You may need to drag the column boundaries to a position so that the labels are displayed sensibly.

5. To enter 'For Office Use Only' you will need to widen the first column on this row only.

6. Select the appropriate cell.

7. Drag the column boundary to accommodate the text.

8. When you have completed this first part of the table, move the cursor below the table, press *Enter* to insert a row, and insert a further table with **Table-Insert Table**, immediately below the first table. This table should have six columns of approximately equal width. You may need to drag the column widths to align the two tables. In addition you should delete any space between the two tables.

9. Enter the final text into this table.

10. Format all of the labels by displaying them in bold.

11. Save as *Application Form*. This document will be improved later.

Table formatting

The table formatting command **Table-Table Properties** allows you to format your table.

❏ The **Table** tab sets the position of the table on the page and the way in which text flows around it.

❏ The **Row** tab covers many aspects of table formatting, including:

- The height of the row

- Whether a multi-line row can be split over two pages

- Whether the table headings are to be repeated if the table splits over two pages

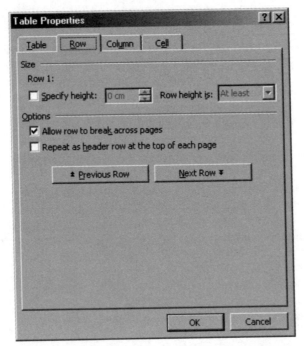

❏ The **Column** tab allows you to specify width of columns for each column in turn.

❏ The **Cell** tab setst the alignment and widths of individual cells. Click on the **Options** button and change the cell margins.

These commands, together with other formatting that is available for all text, offer a wide range of options. To view the effect of formatting on the table, do not forget to view your document in Page Layout view.

Task 2: Formatting a table

1. View *Application Form* in Page Layout view.

2. Select the table.

3. Using **Table-Table Properties** and the **Cell** tab, change the **Vertical Alignment** to **Center**.

4. Select the whole table and, using **Table-Table Properties** and the **Row** tab, set the row height to 0.8cm. Save the document as *Application Form*.

Putting existing text into a table

If you already have a table laid out using tab characters, or some columns of text separated by commas, this can be converted into a table by:

1. Selecting the original table

2. Choosing **Table-Convert-Text to Table**

Word will examine the existing text and convert it into a table with suitable column widths.

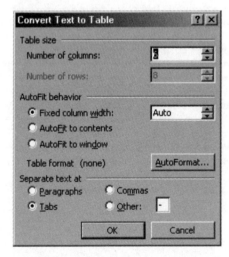

If Word cannot determine how to convert the text, it displays a dialog box listing different conversion options.

If the resultant table is not as you would like it, remember to use **Edit-Undo** before taking any other action.

Alternatively, a table may be converted into regular text paragraphs. Simply select the rows of the table to be converted to text, and choose **Table-Convert-Table to Text**. Select an appropriate **Separate text with** option and click on **OK**.

Task 3: Turning text into tables

This task converts the text in the document *Health Suite Times* into a table.

1. Open the document *Health Suite Times*. This has existing tab stops.

2. Select the section showing opening times for the Health Suite.

3. Click on the ¶ button to display the hidden characters and check that there are only two tabs on each row. Remove any extras. Turn off the display of hidden characters.

4. Choose **Table-Convert Text to Table**. Click on **Tabs** in the **Separate text at** section. The **Number of columns** should show as 3.

5. Click on **OK**. The text should appear as a table with the cell borders displayed.

6. You may need to drag the column boundaries so that the text is all displayed in the most effective way. You may also improve the formatting.

Monday	9.00am - 9.00pm	Ladies Only
Tuesday	9.00am - 9.00pm	Mixed
Wednesday	9.30am - 9.00pm	Mixed
Thursday	9.00am - 1.00pm	Ladies Only
	1.00pm - 9.00pm	Mixed
Friday	9.00am - 9.00pm	Men Only
Saturday	9.00am - 1.00pm	Men Only
	1.00pm - 5.00pm	Mixed
Sunday	9.00am - 5.00pm	Mixed

7. Repeat for the other tables.

8. Save the document as *Health Suite Times2*.

Task 4: Designing a simple questionnaire

You can now start to design a simple questionnaire and to be a little more ambitious in our use of tables. The questionnaire that is to be designed is shown below.

Chelmer Leisure and Recreation Centre
Market Research Questionnaire

Occupation		Sex (M/F)	
Age Band		**Smoking**	
Under 20		Non-smoker	
21-30		Pipe and/or cigar	
31-40		Under 10 cigs a day	
41-50		20 cigs a day	
51-60		30 cigs a day	
Over 60			

Which of the following would you be interested in attending? (Please tick)	*Not at all*	*Somewhat*	*Very much*
Workshops on:			
Diet/Nutrition			
Stress Management			
Exercise			
Health Screening:			
Coronary Risk Assessment			
Cholesterol Check			
Blood Pressure Check			
Flexibility			
Strength			
Dietary Analysis			
Aerobic Fitness			

Please return this questionnaire to Chelmer Leisure and Recreation Centre. Thank you for your co-operation.

1. Open a new document.

2. Type in the title, format and centre it.

3. Place the insertion point on a new line and choose **Table-Insert-Table**, and create a table with four columns.

4. Enter the text in the table down to 'Over 60', using the *Tab* key to move between cells.

5. Press the *Tab* key a few times to create a few empty cells. Leave one blank row.

6. Select these empty cells and drag the column boundaries on the bottom part of the table so that the cells will accommodate the text.

7. Enter the text in the lower part of the table into the new cells.

8. Format the text as appropriate.

9. Save the document as *Market Research Questionnaire*.

Applying Borders and Shading

What you will learn in this unit

This unit introduces the use of borders and shading. The first few tasks help you to learn how to apply borders and shading to plain text. Later in the unit we attempt some much more sophisticated use of borders and shading when we seek to apply them to text in tables. Borders and shading are very useful for enhancing the appearance of a document, or for highlighting specific parts of the document. At the end of this unit you will be able to:

❑ Use Table AutoFormat to apply quick borders and shading.

❑ Apply and format borders to text.

❑ Remove and change borders.

❑ Apply borders to text in tables.

❑ Apply shading to text.

❑ Apply shading to text in tables.

What you need

To complete this unit you will need:

❑ The document file *Address* created in Unit 16

❑ The document file *Open Day* created in Unit 5

❑ The document file *Application Form* created in Unit 17

❑ The document file *Market Research Questionnaire* created in Unit 17.

❑ The document file *Timetable* created in Unit 11.

Applying borders and shading to text

You will have observed that both the form and the questionnaire designed in Unit 17 require additional formatting. This can be achieved by the use of borders and shading.

The design of a document can be improved significantly if borders, lines and shading are used sparingly. Borders and shading can be applied to paragraphs of text, graphics or the cells in a table. With a colour printer, you can print coloured borders and shading. This unit introduces the basics of borders and shading and leaves you to experiment further with the immense potential of these features.

Quick borders and shading: Table AutoFormat

A quick way to apply borders and shading to a table is to use **Table-Table AutoFormat**, which displays the Table AutoFormat dialog box. This dialog box lists a series of preset formats, and shows their format through a Preview box. These preset formats can be modified by changing borders, shading, font, colour and AutoFit. It is also possible to apply special formats to heading rows, first column, last row and last column.

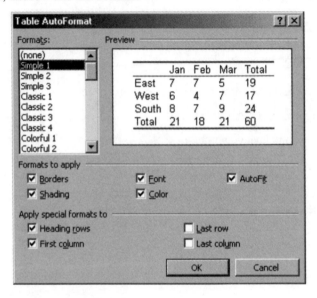

Task 1: Using Table AutoFormat

1. Open the document *Address*.

2. Select the table.

3. Choose **Table-AutoFormat**.

4. Experiment with the different standard formats, until the table resembles the table below. Save the new form.

Supplier	Address	Telephone
Universal Gym (Europe) Ltd	Hutton, Brentwood, Essex CM13 1XA	01277 221122
Atlanta Sports Industries Ltd	Atlanta House, Rotherway, Euroway Estate, Maltby, Rotherham, S66 8QN	01709 700555
Physique Training Equipment Ltd	Bankfield Mill, Greenfield, Road, Come, Lancashire, BB8 9PD	01282 863300

Applying and formatting borders

To apply a border, select the items to which a border is to be applied, then choose **Format-Borders and Shading**. This displays the Borders and Shading dialog box. If no text is selected, but the insertion point is in normal text, the border is applied to the paragraph that contains the insertion point.

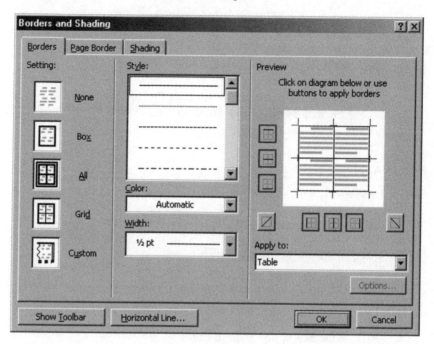

❏ To apply a box, click on the box option under **Setting** and then click a line style under **Style**. If you want to change the colour of the border, select a colour in the **Color** box.

❏ To create a custom border or to add lines within a box, click the border **Preview** where you want to apply a border or one of the border buttons within the **Preview**, and then click a line style under **Style**.

❏ To change the distance of the border from the text click on the **Options** button. Set the distance using the options in the Border and Shading Options dialog box.

❏ To change the width of a border, click on the **Width** box, and select an appropriate width from the options displayed.

Alternatively, click on the **Border** button on the toolbar to display the Borders list.

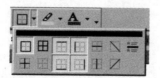

Removing and changing borders

To remove or change a border, first select the item that has the border to be removed or changed. Choose **Format-Borders and Shading**. Then:

❑   To remove all borders, click **None** under **Setting**.

❑   To remove one border at a time, click the border you want to remove on the border sample.

Click on **OK** when you are satisfied with the borders.

Borders may also be changed by selecting the item with the border to be changed. Choose **Format-Borders and Shading**, and change the selected options in the Borders dialog box.

Task 2: Applying borders

This task explores some of the basics of applying borders to text.

1.   Open the document *Open Day*, that you created in Task 1 of Unit 5.

2.   Select all the text in this document.

3.   Choose **Format-Borders and Shading** to display the Borders and Shading dialog box.

4.   Click on the **Box** option under **Setting**.

5.   Choose a line style – e.g. double – under **Style**.

6.   Click on the **Shadow** box.

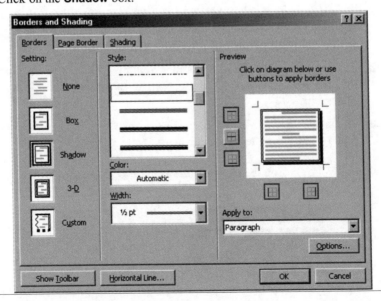

7. Click on **Options**. Increase the spacing to 6pt at the top and bottom of the text.

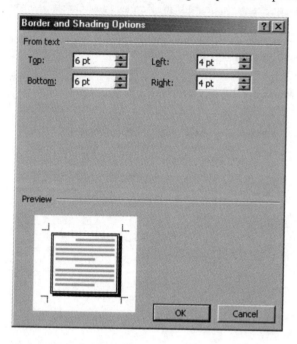

8. Click on **OK** in each dialog box.

> ## CHELMER LEISURE AND RECREATION CENTRE
> ## *AEROBICS OPEN DAY*
>
> **Step**   One of the best ways to start your fitness programme.
>   Our fitness demonstrators will be on hand to advise you
>   on a suitable fitness programme.
>
> **Cycle**   Tone up those flabby thighs and strengthen those backs.
>   Our cycles simulate real cycling conditions, which can
>   be individually tailored to your fitness programme.
>
> **Row**   Fancy yourself in the boat race? Try your hand at our
>   computer controlled rowing machine.

9. Print, and save your document as *Open Day*.

Task 3: Using borders on forms

This task attempts a more sophisticated use of borders for applications such as an application form or questionnaire.

1. Open the document *Application Form*.

2. Ensure that only the gridlines and text are displayed, and no borders.

3. Select the three blank cells to the right of *Name* and convert them into a single cell using **Table-Merge Cells**. Repeat for the *Address* and *Office Use* rows.

4. Select the cells containing 'Sporting' and 'Interests' and merge them. Repeat for the two cells to the right.

5. Make the text in the top portion of the form bold.

Chelmer Leisure and Recreation Centre
Health and Fitness Club
Membership Application Form

Name	
Address	

	Telephone	
Occupation	**Date of Birth**	
Sporting Interests	**Date of Joining**	

For Office Use Only	

Date Subs Due	Subs Paid	Mem.Cat

---

6. Create borders around the cells in which data is to be entered, by selecting each cell in turn and clicking on the ▦▾ button (if necessary, click on the down arrow to select from the borders palette). Alternatively, use **Format-Borders and Shading**.

7. Click on the *Office Use* cell and select **Table-Insert-Rows Above**.

8. Use **Format-Paragraph**, **Format-Font** and **Table-Table Properties** to make the new row very thin.

9. Select the whole row containing 'For Office Use Only'.

10. Choose **Format-Borders and Shading**.

11. Select the top border by clicking on it on the sample.

12. Select a double line under **Style**, then click on the top border again (so that the double line is applied). Click on **OK**.

13. Select the bottom row.

14. Select **Format-Borders and Shading**. Click on **Grid** under **Setting** and choose an appropriate line. Click on **OK**.

15. Choose **Table-Hide Gridlines** and turn off the gridlines so that you can view your formatting and borders. Save the form.

Chelmer Leisure and Recreation Centre
Health and Fitness Club
Membership Application Form

| Name | |
| Address | |

	Telephone	
Occupation	Date of Birth	
Sporting Interests	Date of Joining	

For Office Use Only

| Date Subs Due | | Subs Paid | | Mem.Cat | |

Applying shading

Shading can be applied to paragraphs or the cells in a table. If you have a colour printer, you can shade tables and paragraphs with colours.

Shading can be used to shade a short section in a newsletter, or an important column of figures in a table. Shading on paragraphs covers the text. Shading in tables fills the cell.

Remember that shading affects the legibility of the text. In general, light shading of 20% or less is most effective. Small font sizes are difficult to read with shading. The use of bold may improve the text legibility.

Choose **Format-Borders and Shading** and click on the **Shading** tab. The Shading dialog box (illustrated below) has the following options:

Fill	Click on one of these boxes to select a colour for the shading.
Patterns-Style	Click on one of these options to choose the density or style of shading.
Patterns-Color	Click on one of these options to select a colour for the pattern in the shading.

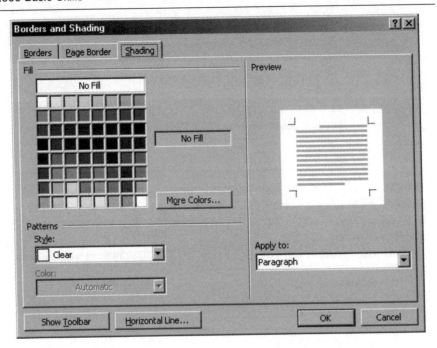

Task 4: Applying shading

This task improves the questionnaire that was designed in Unit 17 by adding borders and shading. This is a relatively ambitious project and although the basic steps are outlined below you are likely to find that parts of the tables have moved to places where you do not want them. You need to be confident in working with tables to succeed with this task.

Open the *Market Research Questionnaire* document. To add borders and shading to the questionnaire:

1. Select the first two lines, i.e. the heading.

2. Select **Format-Borders and Shading**, choose an appropriate double-line box and click on **Shadow**. Click on **OK**.

3. Remove all borders from the table. Show the gridlines.

4. The top two sets of boxes would look better if they were separated. Select the top part of the third column and insert a column using **Table-Insert-Cells** and choosing **Shift cells right**.

5. With the top part of the table selected move the column boundary to make this new column fairly narrow.

6. Select each set of boxes with labels and associated reply boxes and apply a single line border with the **Grid** option.

7. Now apply shading to the cells containing headings, as shown in the example below. In each case, select the cell, choose **Format-Borders and Shading** and then click on the **Shading** tab. Choose a **Shading**, say **20%**. Experiment with a style for your shading. Click on **OK**.

Chelmer Leisure and Recreation Centre Market Research Questionnaire		

Occupation		**Sex (M/F)**	

Age Band		**Smoking**	
Under 20		Non-smoker	
21-30		Pipe and/or cigar	
31-40		Under 10 cigs a day	
41-50		20 cigs a day	
51-60		30 cigs a day	
Over 60			

Which of the following would you be interested in attending? (Please tick)	*Not at all*	*Somewhat*	*Very much*
Workshops on:			
Diet/Nutrition			
Stress Management			
Exercise			
Health Screening:			
Coronary Risk Assessment			
Cholesterol Check			
Blood Pressure Check			
Flexibility			
Strength			
Dietary Analysis			
Aerobic Fitness			

Please return this questionnaire to Chelmer Leisure and Recreation Centre. Thank you for your co-operation.

8. Put a box around the final paragraph.

9. Hide the gridlines. Save your document as *Market Research Questionnaire* and print it.

Special tips for borders and shading

The ways in which you can apply borders and shading are almost endless. Here are just a few ideas that might be useful.

❑   Word applies borders to the edges of a selected graphic. If you have cropped close to the image and need to add space between the image and the border, select the graphic to display the sizing handles. Press *Shift* and drag the centre handles on each side of the graphic to increase the space between the edge of the graphic and the image.

❑   To place graphics adjacent to one another place the graphics in a table, and then apply borders to the table cells.

❑   To add a double border to separate column headings from table entries first apply single borders on all sides of the cell. Select the table, choose **Format-Borders and Shading** and under **Setting** select **Grid**, then click on **OK**. Select the first row of the table and change the line style of the border below the row.

❑   You can apply borders to paragraphs and graphics within a table cell in addition to the borders that you apply to the cell itself.

❑   If you want to apply the same border to a group of paragraphs, all paragraphs must have the same indents. Otherwise paragraphs are placed in separate boxes. To place all text in one box, convert the text to a one-column table.

Task 5: Using borders and shading

In this task we wish to create the table below, which summarises a timetable for activities at the leisure centre during the week.

1. Open the document *Timetable*, created in Unit 11.

2. Mark the text in the body of the table and use **Table-Convert-Text to Table** to create a 6-column table.

3. Change the font throughout to Arial.

4. Make the columns a reasonable width and add space above and below the text. Centre the text in the cells in the main part of the table.

5. Select the table, and apply borders using **Format-Borders and Shading**. Apply a **Grid** where appropriate.

Chelmer Leisure and Recreation Centre ACTIVITY PROGRAMME					
FITNESS SUITE	**Monday**	**Tuesday**	**Wednesday**	**Thursday**	**Friday**
Daytime					
10.00-11.00 am	Ladies Aerobics	Mens Multi-gym	Ladies Aerobics		Body Conditioning
11.00-12.00 pm	Weight Training			Weight Training	Step Aerobics
2 .00-3.00 pm		Ladies Multi-gym	Body Conditioning	Step Aerobics	Mens Multi-gym
3.00-4.00 pm	Body Conditioning		Weight Training	Multi-gym	
Evening					
7.00-9.00 pm	Step Aerobics	Family Multi-gym	Weight Training	Body Conditioning	

6. Select the heading cells and apply shading using **Format-Borders and Shading**. (Remember that you can change several cells at once.)

7. Save the document as *Timetable*.

Task 6: Creating a questionnaire

The following task uses a table to set up a simple questionnaire. It is printed in two formats below, one that shows the completed questionnaire and another that demonstrates the way in which a table has been used to create the questionnaire.

You should now be able to set up an appropriate table, apply borders and enter the text without any additional instructions. Save the document as *IT Questionnaire*.

Chelmer Leisure and Recreation Centre
Staff Workshops in IT

It is planned to run some staff development workshops in IT, during a week in the near future. If you are interested in attending sessions please indicate your area of interest in the following questionnaire.

These sessions could be run in two forms:

1.   General introduction to software, to introduce IT skills.

2.   A more user-oriented approach aimed primarily at experimenting with your ideas and to judge how to make use of the facilities available to you.

Please return completed forms to the IT Co-ordinator.

Name:

Please tick those areas of interest

Introducing IT skills

Introducing Windows 3.1   ☐

Introduction to Word Processing using Microsoft Word   ☐

Introduction to Graphics using Microsoft Word   ☐

Introduction to Spreadsheets using Microsoft Excel   ☐

Introduction to Databases using Microsoft Access   ☐

Using IT in your area of work

Word Processing   ☐

Spreadsheets   ☐

Graphics   ☐

Please indicate below if you feel that there are any other areas of IT you wish to investigate:

Chelmer Leisure and Recreation Centre
Staff Workshops in IT

It is planned to run some staff development workshops in IT, during a week in the near future. If you are interested in attending sessions please indicate your area of interest in the following questionnaire.

These sessions could be run in two forms:

1. General introduction to software, to introduce IT skills.

2. A more user-oriented approach aimed primarily at experimenting with your ideas and to judge how to make use of the facilities available to you.

Please return completed forms to the IT Co-ordinator.

Name:

Please tick those areas of interest

Introducing IT skills

Introducing Windows 3.1	
Introduction to Word Processing using Microsoft Word	
Introduction to Graphics using Microsoft Word	
Introduction to Spreadsheets using Microsoft Excel	
Introduction to Databases using Microsoft Access	

Using IT in your area of work

Word Processing	
Spreadsheets	
Graphics	

Please indicate below if you feel that there are any other areas of IT you wish to investigate:

Adding Pictures

What you will learn in this unit

Word allows a graphic image to be created and inserted into a document. Graphic images are integral parts of many documents and the drawing toolbar offers a means to construct them from within the word processor.

In this unit the basic features of the drawing toolbar are explored. At the end of this unit you should be able to:

❑ Create basic shapes from which images can be created.

❑ Create simple images and diagrams.

❑ Import pictures from other applications.

Drawings are invaluable in many documents, for example in presenting plans or layouts. Box and line diagrams are widely used in many scientific and technical documents.

In Word there are two types of image, those that 'float' over the text and those that do not, known as *in-line* images. Images that 'float' over text are not displayed in Normal view; they are only displayed in Page Layout view. In-line images can be seen in both Normal and Page Layout view. Floating images are more flexible in the ways in which they can be positioned on the page but can be a little tricky to work with. They are the default type of image.

Displaying the Drawing toolbar

The Drawing toolbar can be displayed by clicking on the 🔧 button in the standard toolbar. (Click on ⁑ to display more buttons if you can't see the button.)

Alternatively, select **View-Toolbars** and click on **Drawing**.

The drawing toolbar is displayed at the bottom of the screen but can be dragged elsewhere. The drop-down lists and buttons on the toolbar are the drawing tools and functions.

Drawings can be created either directly in Page Layout view or they can be created as a separate picture.

In Page Layout view you may draw directly on the text on your document. The drawing can remain fixed at that position on the page or it can be anchored to a paragraph so that it will move with the text. This sort of drawing is a floating image that is only visible in Page Layout view.

A drawing may be created as a separate picture and for diagrams in a document this is the best method. The picture can be left as a floating image or changed into an in-line image that is also visible in Normal view. To create a picture, select **Insert-Object** and choose **Microsoft Word Picture**. A drawing workspace is displayed, with an Edit Picture toolbar.

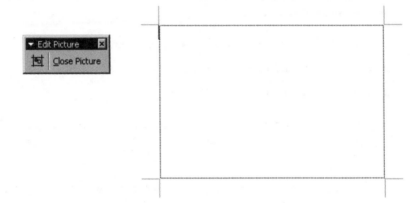

You can create your picture within the boundary shown, or if your drawing element is outside the boundary click on the ⊡ button in the Edit Picture box to enclose all drawing elements in the picture boundary. When the picture is complete click on the **Close Picture** button to return to your document.

To edit a picture in a document simply double-click on it to display it in the drawing workspace.

Creating basic shapes

To draw lines click on the ＼ (**Line**) button, position the pointer at the start of the line, click and drag to the end of the line. Lines may be freely positioned or they may start and end on invisible grid points. The following task investigates how the **Snap to Grid** feature on the drawing toolbar can be used to control this.

Task 1: Drawing lines

Start a new document and click on the ⬮ button to display the Drawing toolbar. Select **Insert-Object** and choose **Microsoft Word Picture** to display the drawing workspace. Note that all the tasks will create drawings as separate entities but if you wish you may draw directly on your document in Page Layout view.

1. Click on the line-drawing tool. In the drawing area the pointer changes to a +.

2. Position the pointer near the top of the area enclosed by the drawing boundary, click and drag towards the bottom of the drawing area. Don't release the mouse button just yet; notice how the line follows your pointer movements in a rather jerky fashion.

3. Release the mouse button and a line is drawn.

4. Click on the **Draw** button on the drawing toolbar and choose **Grid**. This displays the Drawing Grid dialog box.

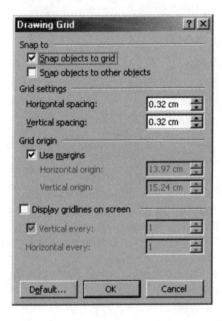

Notice that the **Snap objects to grid** check box is ticked. This is the reason for the jerkiness of the line positioning. When **Snap objects to grid** is on lines start and finish at invisible grid points. This is useful for maintaining consistency in a drawing. Through the Drawing Grid dialog box the spacing of the invisible grid can be customised.

5. Remove the tick in the **Snap to grid** check box and repeat the line-drawing exercise. This time notice that the end of the line should follow your pointer movements smoothly.

6. Experiment with drawing lines of different thickness and style. Different line styles may be selected by clicking on the ≡ (**Line Style**) button in the toolbar. You can select from the menu of styles or the Format AutoShape dialog box can be displayed by clicking on **More Lines**. This provides even more options.

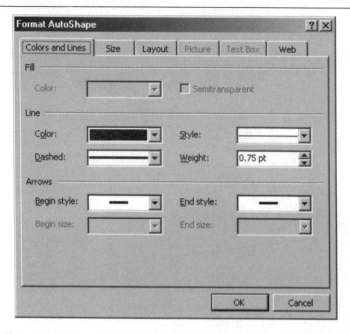

7. Change the size and angle of lines by clicking on them and then dragging the end markers.

8. Click on the **Close Picture** button to return to the document. Select the picture by clicking on it and choose **Format-Object**. Select the **Layout** tab and check that the **In line with text box** is selected. Floating images will be considered in more detail in a later unit. You can also use the Picture toolbar to make these changes.

9. Save the document as *Doodle*. Once a drawing is embedded in a document it can be manipulated in the same way as an embedded chart, i.e. its size can be changed and it may be cut, copied and pasted.

Drawing ellipses, circles, rectangles and squares

The methods for drawing these shapes are summarised in the following table:

Ellipse/circle ⬭	Rectangle/square ▢	
To draw an ellipse from the corner of an imaginary bounding box	*To draw a rectangle from one corner*	Click on appropriate tool icon, position pointer at corner and drag to size required.
To draw an ellipse from its centre	*To draw a rectangle from its centre*	Click on appropriate tool icon, hold down the *Ctrl* key, position pointer at centre and drag to size required.

To draw a circle from the corner of an imaginary bounding box	*To draw a square from one corner*	Click on appropriate tool icon, hold down the *Shift* key, position pointer at centre and drag to size required.
To draw a circle from its centre	*To draw a square from its centre*	Click on appropriate tool icon, hold down the *Ctrl* and *Shift* keys, position pointer at centre and drag to size required.

A shadowed object can be constructed by clicking on the ▣ (**Shadow**) button in the Drawing toolbar and selecting the type of shadow required.

The ▣ (**3D**) button converts a rectangle or ellipse into a 3-dimensional object.

Similar effects can be achieved with the ◣ tool.

Autoshapes

To draw shapes other than rectangles and ellipses, click on the **Autoshapes** button in the Drawing toolbar. This displays a menu of different shapes from which you can choose.

Task 2: Creating basic shapes

1. Open the document *Doodle*, position the pointer in the drawing and double-click. This displays your drawing in the picture workspace and allows the chosen drawing to be updated.

2. Create each of the shapes described in the preceding table. Experiment with the AutoShapes and shadows. Explore the effect that snap to grid has on the way in which the shapes are created.

3. Change the size of shapes by clicking on them and then dragging the sizing handles on the edges and corners.

4. Some of your shapes may go outside the drawing boundary. If so, click on the ▣ button.

5. Save this drawing by clicking on **Close Picture** and using **File-Save** for revision in later tasks.

    Note: To draw a rectangle or ellipse several times, double-click on the tool you require. When you finish, click anywhere in the document to deselect the drawing tool.

Drawing arcs

You can draw 90° segments (quadrants) of ellipses or circles by selecting **AutoShapes-Basic Shapes** and clicking on the ◠ button.

Once the arc has been drawn it can be stretched or shrunk by dragging either end.

Task 3: Drawing arcs

For this task open the drawing from the document *Doodle* and add an arc to it.

1. Select the ◠ (**Arc**) drawing tool from **AutoShapes-Basic Shapes**. Position the pointer at one end of where the arc is to begin.

2. Drag to complete the arc. The direction in which the dragging is done determines which quadrant of an ellipse is drawn. If an arc of a circle is required hold down the *Shift* key during the dragging operation.

3. Click on the arc to select it and drag the white sizing handles to change the size. Drag the yellow handles to change the angle of the arc.

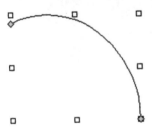

4. Close the picture and save the document *Doodle*.

Drawing freeform shapes

Shapes composed of straight lines and/or freehand lines can be drawn using the ◠ (**Freeform**) button available in the **Lines** group of **AutoShapes**. A freeform shape may be closed, i.e. the beginning and the end of the shape join up, or it may be open. A closed shape can be filled with a colour and/or pattern.

Drawing a shape composed of straight lines

Click on the ⌁ (**Freeform**) tool, position the pointer at the start of the shape, click, move the pointer to the end of the first line, click and repeat for each line in the shape. If the shape is to be closed, click for the last time near the beginning of the first line.

To create an open shape, when it is finished press *Enter* or *Esc* or double-click.

Drawing a freehand shape

Click on the ⌁ (**Freeform**) tool, position the pointer at the start of the shape, click and drag to draw the shape. Do not worry if your drawing is shaky or inaccurate, Word offers the facility to edit the drawing, as described in the next unit.

An open or closed shape may be created as for a shape composed of straight lines.

Drawing a shape with both freehand and straight line sections

It is possible to alternate between drawing a straight line or drawing freehand to produce a composite shape. Use the move and click technique for drawing straight lines and a click and drag technique for the freehand sections. Open or closed shapes may be created.

Task 4: Creating an image

The techniques just described will be experimented with in a new picture. The aim is to reproduce the image shown below. This image is composed of a closed shape (the C), an open shape (the L) and an AutoShape (the star).

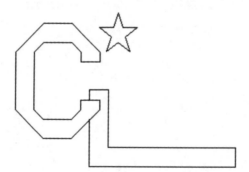

1. Start a new document and click on the button to display the Drawing toolbar. Select **Insert-Object** and choose **Microsoft Word Picture** to display the drawing workspace.

2. Click on the **AutoShapes** button and choose the five-point star tool from the **Stars and Banners** group. Click and drag a star in the picture workspace.

3. Click on the **AutoShapes** button and choose the **Freeform** tool from the **Lines** group. Draw the 'C' shape by positioning the pointer at the start of the shape and clicking and dragging to draw the shape.

4. Finish the shape at the original start position so that a closed shape is formed.

5. To create the 'L' start at the 'C', work down to the bottom, along, and then back up. Experiment with combining freehand and straight lines to create this shape.

6. As this is an open shape, end the shape by double-clicking.

7. Close the picture and save the document as *CLC Logo*. Preview and print it.

Importing pictures

As well as the clipart files supplied with Word, files containing pictures can be created by other applications. A picture file can be imported directly into a document using **Insert-Picture** or can be imported into a picture workspace in the same way. Two common types of picture file that are created by other Windows applications are formatted as either a bitmap or a Windows metafile. Other formats as well as these may be imported: for example, .gif and .jpg formats used for pictures in Web pages.

A bitmap stores the image as being made up of many tiny squares known as pixels. Other formats store the image as being made up of objects such as lines,

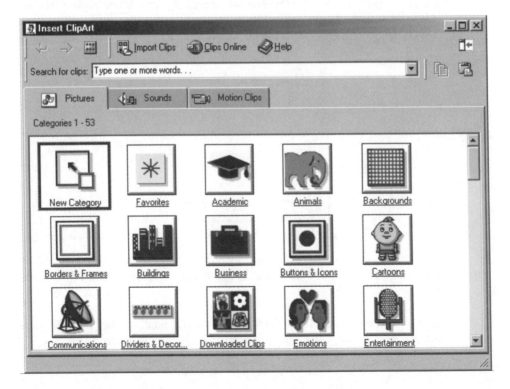

ellipses and rectangles, Word is able to 'decode' this information, so enabling more flexibility for editing the imported image.

To insert a clipart picture use **Insert-Picture-Clip Art**. The Insert ClipArt dialog box appears (as illustrated above).

Select the category you require, scroll through the clipart images until you find a suitable image, select it and click on the **Insert clip** button.

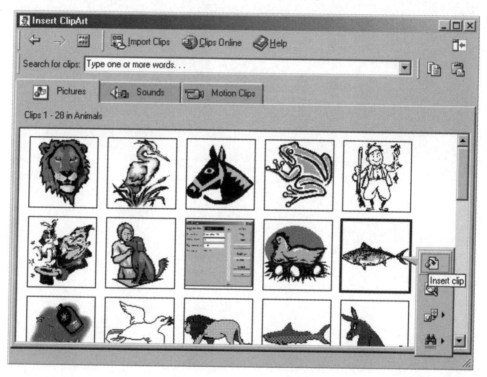

Note that clip art images are inserted as in-line images but you may convert them to floating images.

To insert a picture from a file use **Insert-Picture-From File** and the Insert Picture dialog box appears (see below).

In the **Look in** box, select the folder (directory) in which the picture file is situated. From the **Name** box select the file required. All picture files that Word recognises will be listed in the **Name** box. After selecting the file click on **Insert** and the file will be imported into the document or drawing workspace.

If **Float over text** is checked the picture will be inserted as a floating image, otherwise as an in-line image.

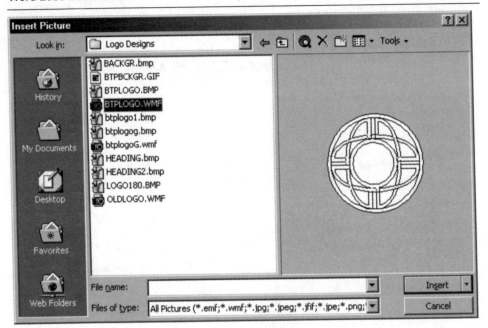

Editing Pictures

What you will learn in this unit

This unit continues from the previous one by examining ways in which images may be edited. At the end of the unit you will be able to:

❑ Edit previously created images.

❑ Add text to images.

Word can import pictures from a variety of sources, so whether you wish to incorporate some clipart or a scanned image into your document the process is simple. A company logo or a cartoon, for example, can easily be incorporated into a document.

What you need

To complete this unit you will need:

❑ The document file *CLC Logo* created in Unit 19.

Editing an image

It is very unlikely that a drawing will be right first time and parts of it will need to be altered or removed. An image is usually made of several parts. A different drawing tool may have been used to create each part or there may be several parts created by the same tool. Each part of the drawing is known as an *object*. Each object may be selected and altered individually or objects may be selected together.

To edit a picture, double-click on it.

Selecting objects: arrow tool

The object that needs to be altered or deleted must be selected before changes can be made. Click on the ⟋ button on the Drawing toolbar to change the pointer to an arrow for selecting the required object.

Use the arrow to click on the object that is to be altered. If the object is filled then you may point to anywhere within the bounds of the object; if it is not filled then point to the outside edge of the object. The pointer changes shape to a four-headed arrow.

If the object is a line, clicking will cause a handle (small white box) to appear at each end. For other objects eight handles will appear. These handles are at the corners and the middle of the sides of an invisible rectangle surrounding the object.

The handles are known as *sizing handles* and can be used to edit the object.

Selecting more than one object

If the same editing action is to be performed on more than one object of the image, then more than one object can be selected. First consider where an imaginary box that would enclose all of the objects required would be. Using the arrow, point to one corner of this imaginary box and click and drag. A dotted line box appears. Make sure you have surrounded all the objects you wish to select, before releasing the mouse button.

An alternative method is to select each object in turn while holding down the *Shift* key.

Removing parts of an image

Select the objects to be removed. By using **Edit-Clear** or pressing the *Delete* key the selected objects will be removed. Don't forget that you can use **Edit-Undo** if this goes wrong!

Moving and copying

Any object or group of objects can be moved from one location to another in a drawing. To move a single object, select it and then drag the four-headed arrow pointer to the new position. A *ghost* (a dotted outline of the object) will move across the screen as you move the mouse. Release the mouse button to drop the object in its new place.

To move a group of objects, first select the objects required. Click on any one of the objects in the group and then drag as for a single object.

Any object or group of objects can be copied using the normal copy-and-paste operation. First select the object or objects to be copied, use **Edit-Copy** and follow with **Edit-Paste**. A copy will be pasted into the drawing and can be moved to the appropriate place.

Task 1: Copy and paste

Open the *CLC Logo* document created in Task 4 of Unit 19 and double-click on the picture.

1. Select the 'C' by clicking anywhere inside it.

2. Using **Edit-Copy** and **Edit-Paste** make a copy of the 'C'.

3. Move the copy by dragging it to the right-hand side of the picture as illustrated below. (**Hint**: You may need to turn off **Snap to Grid** temporarily for this action.)

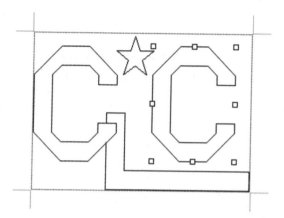

4. Close the picture and save the document.

Resizing an object

To resize an object the sizing handles, which appear when the object is selected, are used. Any one of the handles may be dragged to resize the object, bearing in mind that the object will behave as if it is pinned to the drawing with the opposite corner from the one that is being dragged.

The point at which the object is pinned is known as the *anchor point*. As an alternative to one of the corners of the bounding box being the anchor point, a central anchor point can be chosen. To do this hold down the *Ctrl* key during the resizing operation.

During resizing the object is displayed in the same way as during moving, that is, as a ghost.

Controlling height, width or proportions during resizing

To resize an object so that its proportion of height to width remains the same, hold down the *Shift* key while dragging a sizing handle diagonally.

To resize an object so that its height or width remains unchanged, drag one of the central side handles.

Grouping objects for editing

You may wish to create a composite object which is composed of simpler shapes and then be able to work with the object as one for sizing and moving. Objects may be grouped which reduces the clutter of many sizing handles and also can speed operation as Word works faster with objects that are grouped. To group a set of selected objects click on the **Draw** button and select **Group** from the menu. When you have finished the editing then the objects may be ungrouped using the **Ungroup** option in the **Draw** menu.

Task 2: Resizing

Open the image from the previous task. Select the star. By dragging one of the sizing handles and holding down *Shift*, make it larger, as illustrated below.

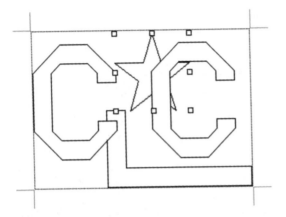

Editing freeform images

All freeform images are composed of lines connected end to end. Even freehand curves are made up of lots of little lines connected end to end. The point at which one line joins to the next is known as a *vertex*.

Before any changes can be made to a freeform it is necessary to display it in editing mode. Select the freeform and choose **Edit points** from the **Draw** menu. The freeform is shown with the vertices marked with little control handles. To see these more clearly it may be necessary to zoom in on your drawing (see below).

By dragging the control handles it is possible to edit the freeform. It may be necessary to check that the Snap to grid option is not checked.

If there are a lot of vertices, some can be deleted. To delete a vertex, position the pointer on the control handle belonging to that vertex, hold down the *Ctrl* key and click. A line will join the remaining vertices either side of the one deleted. To add a vertex, point to the line where a vertex is to be added, hold down the *Ctrl* key and click.

Task 3: Editing a freeform

Open the image from the previous task.

1. Select the 'L' part of the logo.

2. Choose **Edit points** from the **Draw** menu to display the control handles.

3. Drag the control handles to line up the end of the 'L' with the right-hand side of the second 'C'.

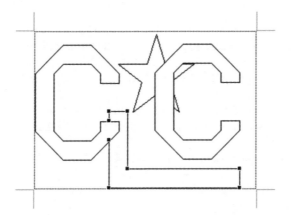

4. Click on 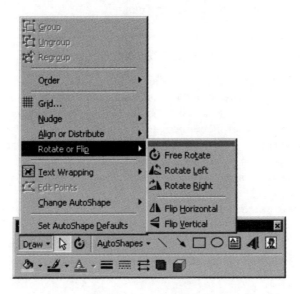 on the Edit Picture toolbar to adjust the image size.

5. Close the drawing and save the document.

Rotating or flipping an object

Rotating causes an object to be rotated through 90° or any other angle and *flipping* causes an object to become its mirror image. Rotating or flipping can be performed on one object or a group of objects. They do not work on text objects or bitmaps. Bitmaps are explained later in this unit.

Select the object or objects to be rotated or flipped and choose **Rotate or Flip** from the **Draw** menu. If rotating choose **Free Rotate**, **Rotate Left** or **Rotate Right** from the menu; if flipping choose either **Flip Horizontal** or **Flip Vertical**. Notice that there is also a **Free Rotate** button in the Drawing toolbar.

Task 4: Rotate and flip

1. Open the previous image and rotate left the 'C' on the left of the drawing.

2. Flip horizontally the 'C' on the right of the drawing.

3. Select the right-hand star and choose **Free Rotate**. You will notice the object is bounded by an imaginary square with a small green circle at each corner.

4. Drag one of the circles to freely rotate the object.

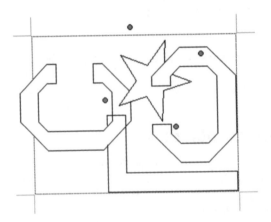

5. Return to the document and close without saving.

Lines and fills; colour and patterns

Objects such as rectangles, ellipses or other shapes can be drawn with or without lines (outside edges) and fills. It is possible to set no fill and no line for an object and it then becomes invisible, so take care when choosing settings. When first drawn an object has a line or fill defined by the settings of the AutoShape defaults. Changes to the defaults can be made by creating an object with the required characteristics and then choosing **Draw-Set AutoShape Defaults**. The new setting affects only objects drawn after changes are made to the defaults.

An object can have different settings from the drawing defaults by double-clicking on the object or choosing **Format-AutoShape** and altering the settings in the **Colors and Lines** tab of the **Format-AutoShape** dialog box.

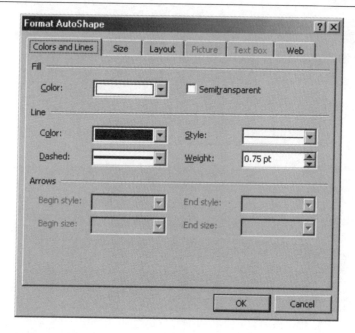

Choosing lines and fills

The style and width of an object's outside line reflect the default settings under the **Colours and Lines** tab of the **Format-AutoShape** dialog box. Line style can be set using the **Line Style**, **Dash Style** and **Arrow Style** buttons on the Drawing toolbar or by choosing **Format-AutoShape**.

An object may be filled. Select the object and click on the **Fill Colour** button in the Drawing toolbar. Select a colour from the colour grid.

Instead of solid colour fills, shading and patterns may be used. Double-click on the object and choose from the options in the **Fill** section of the **Colours and Lines** tab of the **Format-AutoShape** dialog box. Objects may be filled with solid colour, graded colour, patterns, textures and pictures.

Task 5: Filling

1. Continuing with the previous drawing, double-click on an edge of the 'L' object.

2. Choose the **Colours and Lines** tab, open the **Color** drop-down list in the **Line** section and select green.

3. Similarly, select green in the **Color** drop-down list in the **Fill** section.

4. Choose a pattern by opening the **Color** drop-down list in the **Fill** section and choosing **Fill Effects**. Select the **Patterns** tab and choose an appropriate pattern.

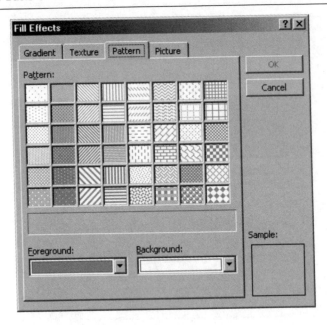

5. Click on **OK**, and **OK** again. You may wish to experiment with different fills and effects. Do not save these changes.

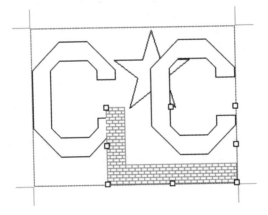

Overlapping objects

If an image is created where one object overlaps another then the most recently drawn object will obscure the earlier object. Word treats the objects as if they are stacked one on top of another, with the most recent on top. This stacking order can be changed by selecting an object and choosing **Draw-Order-Bring to Front** to put the object on top of the stack or **Draw-Order-Bring to Back** to send the object to the bottom of the stack.

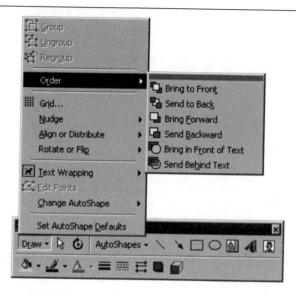

Task 6: Overlapping

1. Open *CLC Logo* and double-click on the picture to edit it.

2. Select the star and move it to the middle of the picture.

3. Send the star to the back of the picture with **Draw-Order-Send to Back**. Save the picture.

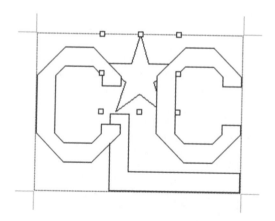

Moving around a drawing: zoom

Choose the level of magnification from the **Zoom** drop-down list box in the main toolbar. There are eight levels of magnification: 10%, 25%, 50%, 75%, 100%, 150%, 200% and 500%, and also **Page Width**, **Text Width**, **Whole Page** and **Two Pages**. If **25%** is chosen the image shown is reduced to a quarter of full size; if **200%** is chosen the image is shown twice full size. Use the scrollbars to display the required portion of the picture on the screen.

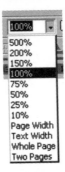

Images and text

The full range of text fonts available to you within Word is also available to a drawing. Headings and labels can easily be part of the drawing. To put text into an image click on the ▣ (**Text box**) button in the Drawing toolbar and click on the picture to create a text box into which you can insert text.

Inside the text box is an insertion point, which is where your text will appear as it is keyed in. When the text is complete simply move on to the next action you wish to perform. While the text box is still selected you can perform text formatting in the usual way. For example, the font, size, colour and alignment of the text can be adjusted.

Editing text

To add or correct text within the text box, click on the text. This places an insertion point in the text, so that additions and corrections can be made.

To change the box around the text, double-click on the edge of the text box and make the necessary selections in the **Colors and Lines** tab. To remove the border, click on **Color** in the **Line** section and choose **No Line**.

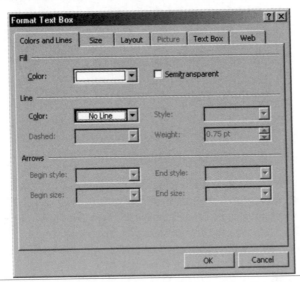

You can also reduce the amount of white space around the text by changing the margins on the **Text Box** tab.

Task 7: Adding text

1. Add the text 'Chelmer' to the drawing as shown. Use 8-point bold Arial text. Set the text border to **No Line** and set the internal margins to 0cm.

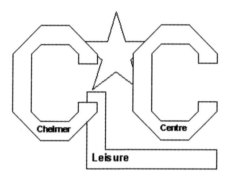

2. Copy the text to the second 'C' and edit it to become 'Centre'.

3. Add 'Leisure' to the 'L' by pasting another copy of the text box and changing the font to 10-point.

4. Save the changes.

Task 8: Images in tables

1. Start a new document and key in the text for the picture below. Add the picture with **Insert-Object-Microsoft Word Picture**. The head is an ellipse and the body is constructed from a series of straight lines. You will need to change the grid spacing to 0.16cm on the **Draw-Grid** dialog box. Close the picture and save the document as *Exercises*.

Starting position for all of these exercises is on all fours. Hands should be placed a shoulder's width apart, knees slightly apart, arms and thighs vertical.

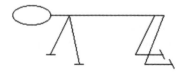

In the next part of the task two images are created side by side by putting them into a table. The first picture will then be added in to the top of the table, creating the document shown below.

Note that when you create drawings in this way you can only achieve very basic results. For a more sophisticated end-product, create the image in a drawing program and then import it into Word.

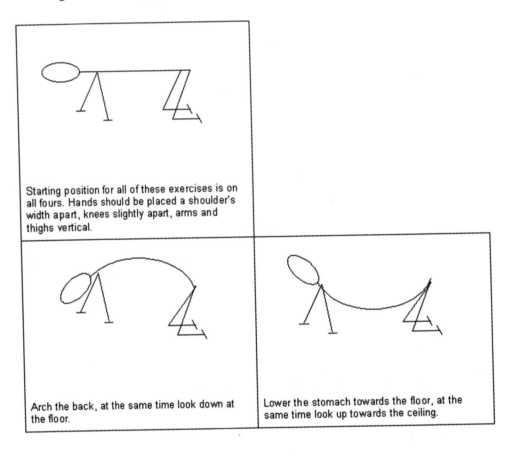

Starting position for all of these exercises is on all fours. Hands should be placed a shoulder's width apart, knees slightly apart, arms and thighs vertical.

Arch the back, at the same time look down at the floor.

Lower the stomach towards the floor, at the same time look up towards the ceiling.

2. Set up a table that is two columns wide and one row deep. Copy and paste the image from step 1 into the first column. Double-click on the image to edit it.

3. Delete the straight line back. Redraw half of the back using the arc tool (in **AutoShapes-Basic shapes**). Start at the midpoint and draw to the neck. Stretch this arc to complete the spine.

4. Rotate the head using **Draw-Rotate or Flip-Free Rotate**. Send the arc to the back of the picture. Group the lines for the arms with **Draw-Group** and move them to their new position. Adjust the legs.

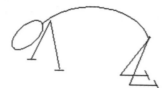

5. Copy the image into the second column. Using **Flip Vertical**, flip the head and the back separately. Select each in turn and move into position. Move the arms and legs as necessary.

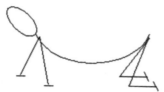

6. Return to the document and save.

7. Add another row to the table in which to put the text associated with each diagram. Put the first picture and its text into new rows at the top of the table. Save the document.

Task 9: A sign

1. Start a new document and switch to Page Layout view. If necessary, click on the button in the main toolbar to display the Drawing toolbar.

2. Click on the button and draw a text box. Choose a thick line for the edge of the box and choose **No Fill**. Add the text, choosing appropriate font, alignment and paragraph spacing.

3. Click on the tool and add a circle. Send it to the back. Save the document as *Fire Door*.

Recreate the same logo using the drawing workspace (**Insert-Object-Microsoft Word Picture**). Investigate the difference between the way Word displays the two signs in Normal and Page Layout views.

Customising Word

Tools-Options

Word can be customised to suit a particular user or the circumstances in which it is being used. This appendix investigates the options available from the **Tools-Options** command. These options are grouped into the following categories:

View	**General**
Edit	**Print**
Save	**Spelling and grammar**
Track changes	**User information**
Compatibility	**File locations**

Not all of these will be discussed: only those options which it is considered the reader may wish to change. To use any of the other options consult the help information to be sure that you know the effect of any change you make.

View

In this category the options available affect the window display, text and non-printing characters.

By clicking in the appropriate check boxes, you can choose whether or not to display the scrollbars and the status bar.

If, in Normal view, the **Style area width** is increased from its default value of zero, the document is displayed with a left margin showing the style name applied to the corresponding text.

It is best to leave the **Formatting marks** options as their default values. There may be occasions when hidden characters such as paragraph marks are required to be seen. However, you will usually switch these on or off with the ¶ button.

General

Here you can alter the measurement units that Word uses. You may choose between centimetres, millimetres, inches, points and picas. You can also specify the number of recently opened files that will be displayed on the **File** menu.

Edit

The one setting you may wish to alter is that of **Typing replaces selection**, particularly if you are new to Word. New users of Word can make selections by

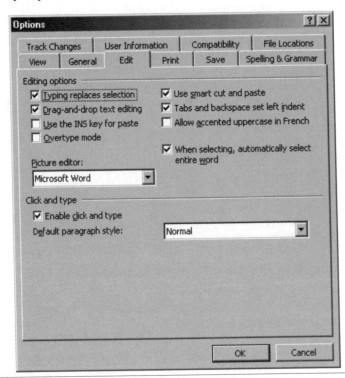

mistake and if this is followed by, say, pressing *Enter* then the selection disappears. (It has been replaced by a paragraph mark.) **Edit-Undo** will remedy this but a new user might not recognise what has happened soon enough. If this option is switched off, by clicking in the check box to remove the tick, then this problem is avoided.

Other settings in this category which you may wish to alter are the operation of the drag and drop feature or the selection of text in units of whole words.

Print

The option in this section you may wish to use is **Reverse print order**. This will cause a document to be printed from the last page to the first, which is useful if your printer places each sheet face up, so that they end up back to front.

Save

Here it is possible to choose fast saving and creating an automatic backup of your document. If you choose to create a backup copy, you will get a *.bak* version of your document each time you save (the previous backup is overwritten each time). However, it is better simply to get into the habit of saving your work every few minutes.

Word also provides an AutoRecovery feature that will regularly save the document. The AutoRecovery version of the file is loaded when you start Word follow a crash of the system. You can adjust the time interval between saves.

Sensitive documents may be password-protected but be cautious using this.

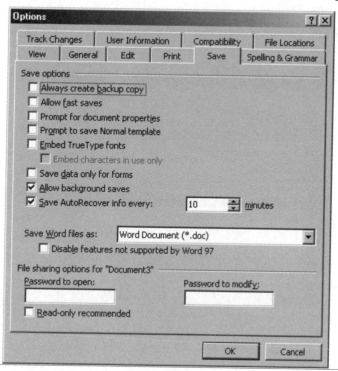

Spelling and Grammar

Word can be customised so that it checks spelling and grammar as you type, depending on these options. Options may be set to allow the spell checker to ignore words that are in upper case, words that contain numbers, etc.

Clicking on the **Dictionaries** button allows you to set up your own dictionary. The **Always suggest corrections** box may be used to speed up checking (checking is quicker if this is switched off). Also, you may choose to check spelling from the main dictionary only.

Track Changes

These options determine the appearance of changes when the tracking feature is turned on (**Tools-Track Changes**).

User Information

Enter your name, initials and address here. Your name is stored with the document each time it is saved.

Compatibility

These options are used if you want to make Word behave like some other word processor (not recommended).

File Locations

The **File Locations** tab allows you to specify the location of specific groups of files.

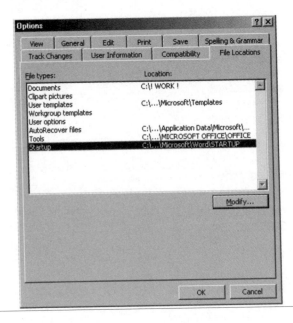

In particular, it is worth setting the **Start** directory to be the folder where you usually store you Word documents. This folder will then be suggested as the default the first time you open or save a document in each Word session.

Customising toolbars

If you find you use a command often, you might want to set up the toolbars so they have precisely the buttons you want to use: for example, adding a button to the Standard toolbar.

To add a button to a toolbar:

1. Choose **View-Toolbars-Customize**.

2. Click on the **Commands** tab, and select a category that includes the button you want to add. The buttons, with their descriptions, appear on the right in a scrollable list box.

3. When you find the button you want to add, drag it and drop it on the toolbar where you want it (at the top of the Word window).

4. Click on Close when you have finished making changes.

You can create your own toolbar by clicking on **New** on the **Toolbars** tab.

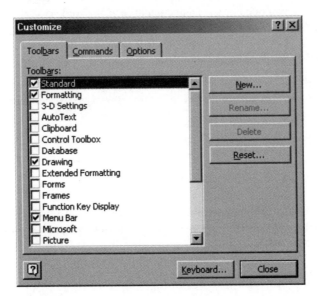

Index